GREG EILERS

Ministering to Transgender Christians

A Resource for the Christian Church

Scripture quotations marked (NIV) are taken from the Holy Bible, New International Version®, NIV®. Copyright © 1973, 1978, 1984, 2011 by Biblica, Inc. Used by permission of Zondervan. All rights reserved worldwide. www.zondervan.comThe "NIV" and "New International Version" are trademarks registered in the United States Patent and Trademark Office by Biblica, Inc.

Foreword © 2020 by Rev. Jon Klein.

Cover design by Alex Eilers.

Cover art by Erin Steedley.

First edition

ISBN: 979-8-6570225-3-7

This book was professionally typeset on Reedsy.
Find out more at reedsy.com

Contents

Foreword

By Rev. Jon Klein

March of 2016—North Carolina issued a "bathroom bill" which banned people from using public bathrooms that don't correspond to the biological sex listed on their birth certificates.

"Well, this is hardly newsworthy," I thought to myself. "You are either male or female. You don't get to choose your gender. There shouldn't be any confusion. Why is this even an issue? Can you even enforce such a bill? Will they have a hall monitor checking people's birth certificates as they try to go to the bathroom? Whatever. That's North Carolina's problem. I'm not going to have to deal with this. I'm a conservative pastor in a church body known for being one of the most conservative churches in the US. I can forget about this whole thing and let the political interest groups duke it out."

Three years later, a dad and a teenager visit my church for the first time. I can tell by how the dad is dressed that he belongs to another faith group. I can tell by his demeanor and his notepad that he's evaluating me and my congregation. I greet them at the end of worship, introducing myself and asking their names. The dad introduces me to his teenage child. I heard the name, and thought, "That's a girl's name. Must be his daughter." I tried to make a little small talk, but he seemed ready to leave. I wished him and his child well.

The next Sunday, the teenager came back by herself. I conversed with her, trying to get to know her. The more she talked, the more I thought, "She has a fairly masculine voice. She's wearing baggy clothes that don't accentuate the shape of the body. Her hair is long. Wait. Is she a girl or a boy? Did I hear the name right last week? Then again, I've known plenty of people whose names work for both boys and girls."

Not wanting to be insensitive or ask a deeply personal question to this person I've only talked to a total of five minutes, I asked a couple of my church members who had interacted with her. Turns out, none of us knew whether she was a boy or a girl.

The pieces came together when one of my members told me they had directed her to the men's restroom only to see her go into the women's.

Oh boy. I thought I would not ever personally deal with this. I have a transgender person coming to my church. What do I do? What do I say? Do I forbid her from going to the bathroom? Do I ask her to leave?

My approach to the situation was my approach to anyone who walks through the doors of my church: love this person. Love this person as Christ loved them. Christ resisted Satan through severe temptation for 40 days having this person in mind. Christ refused to come down from the cross at the taunts of his enemies because he knew that his sacrifice would be the only way this person would be saved. Christ had this person in mind when he said to his disciples, "Go and make disciples of all nations, baptizing them in the name of the Father and of the Son and of the Holy Spirit, and teaching them to obey everything I have commanded you" (Matthew 28:19-20a).

This young person coming to my church all by herself was a blood-bought soul. She needed Christ's forgiveness and salvation and perfection just as much as I did. She was broken by sin as I was broken by sin. God fixes broken people with His perfection lived for us and His sacrificial death died for us. In short: God made me; God saved me. God made her; God saved her.

I thank God that after about two months I got to say those very things to her. At the same time, though, I knew I lacked knowledge and experience on the whole matter of transgender.

My wife and I started researching and doing Bible study specific to the topic of transgender. In doing so, my wife came across a retired Lutheran Church—Missouri Synod (LCMS) pastor who himself is a transgender person. This is how I met Greg Eilers.

My wife and I started reading Greg's blog. In general, I knew the LCMS to be theologically conservative, much like my national church body, the Wisconsin Evangelical Lutheran Synod (WELS). The more I read of his blog posts, the more I felt he and I shared the same biblically-founded faith.

Me, I like to talk to people with experience when it comes to practicing pastoral ministry. I emailed Greg. I laid out my situation. He and I exchanged many emails since.

Not long after my initial conversations with Greg, I learned about his book, *A Roller Coaster Through a Hurricane: One Wild Ride: My Journey with Gender Identity*. I bought it and read it.

I finished it thinking Greg is a pastor much like me. People like Greg, people like the teenager who comes to my congregation, they need people to love them enough to give them Christ, to tell them that in baptism they are clothed with Christ, that their self worth is nothing less than the perfection Jesus lived for them. Greg's Savior, this teenager's Savior, is also my Savior. I rejoice that we share the same Jesus who fulfilled God's Law for all of us and gives the same complete forgiveness to all of us.

Three years ago, gender dysphoria, gender identity issues, and transgender all seemed to me nothing more than deviation from the absolute truth of God's Word by an increasingly atheistic culture and society. Now, I realize this is a real struggle for people. People are spiritually and emotionally hurting as they wrestle with gender dysphoria. People are turning to suicide as their only escape from it.

It may be a minority of people who struggle with gender dysphoria, but God loves all of them just as much as he loves me. It is my prayer that the counsel and direction and experiences from Greg help you love the person who struggles with gender dysphoria so that you can share with them Christ, the Savior of all us messed up people in need of rescue.

Preface

The book-cover art is a painting by my daughter, Erin. It hangs on my wall, above my computer. It often grabs my eye.

Erin created this work when she was in her early twenties. She sought to demonstrate what she was experiencing, the struggle which is her life, and the strength and joy she receives through the love of her Lord Jesus.

It was during Erin's sophomore year of high school that depression snuck into her life. It settled in fast. And hard. Her mother and I learned about the beast which is depression.

People say they battle depression, because that's what it is—a battle. Many days, the depression wins.

It is not pleased with winning one day. It demands many days.

As graduation neared, the depression seized the opportunity to create chaos in Erin's mind over the uncertainty of her future. Three weeks after graduation, she crashed. "Do you think about harming yourself?" "Yes." "Do you know how you would do it?" "Yes."

Erin was suffering so deeply that we could not help her. We admitted her to a hospital.

Where her mother and I had previously only a nominal knowledge of depression, we became immersed in learning about it. We found it to be as malicious and merciless as it is mysterious.

From a young age, Erin exhibited artistic talents, first in song and dance, and then in drawing. These expressions of beauty became her way of counterpunching the ugliness of depression.

She didn't know it at the time, but I immediately saw myself in this particular painting. I asked Erin if I might have it.

My lifetime of struggling with my gender always felt like the chaotic red and death-invoking black of the painting's background. Thankfully, as Erin depicts here with the bright yellow cross, our Lord Jesus' defeat of our mortal enemies never stops shining through to overcome the grim and bleak.

When I began working on this book, jotting ideas for chapters and some specific thoughts, I paused to ponder. My gaze rose above my screen to Erin's painting. Before I completed the book's outline, I knew what the cover art would be.

For Christians quietly suffering gender conflict, the chaotic red and death-invoking black is the constant background of their lives. For those who seek to address their gender issues by speaking aloud their secret, the struggle does not easily resolve. Rather, it moves. From inside to out. From old struggles that had been internal, to new struggles in their homes, on the job, in the community, and in their churches.

They reveal their struggles, but, because they tell of things which are mysterious, the very people they seek for help often become malicious and merciless. Their battle, which they experience so similar to depression, now takes on human form.

It can be hard enough for the love of Jesus to shine when inside chaos and death thrive. It can become impossible when you seek help, desire to be understood, and long for healing, yet those to whom you appeal only muster judgment, contempt, and rejection.

In the last generation, we have come a long way in our understanding of depression, and in our ability to have compassion for those who suffer it.

In this generation, we have a long way to go in making the same progress with gender conflict and for transgender persons.

I pray my daughter's expression of her experience sets a worthy tone for what you will now read.

Acknowledgement

Rev. Rich Tino was one of my good friends in the ministry. When I transitioned to resolve my gender conflict, he did not agree with it, but he kept listening to me. After I experienced the dramatic change that led me to resume living as a male, he agreed there was way more to gender dysphoria and transgender than was being recognized in Christianity.

I kept telling him I longed to educate pastors, church workers, and my fellow Christians. Rich said, "You have to write the book. No one can write it but you. You were a pastor and transgender. You have to write the book."

Thank you, Rich, for your encouragement, and for your ongoing friendship.

Once again, my wife served as my editor. In 2018, when I was in need of a professional set of eyes for my memoir, *A Roller Coaster through a Hurricane*, Julie said, "Let me see that."

Julie received her bachelor's degree in journalism and worked in the past as a journalist. She provided the professional touch my memoir needed. There was no question she would edit this book.

Indeed, I needed her more than ever. My writing style is that of a story teller. Julie is technically proficient. Across the chapters, Julie's expertise provided clarity and depth.

Thank you, My Heart. Who knew we'd one day make as dandy a writing and publishing team as we do a husband and wife?

You read Rev. Jon Klein's foreword. He wrote how we came to be friends. When I completed the first draft of this book, he seemed a natural to read it. He generously gave me his time and thorough feedback, which influenced many topics.

When I was ready for other eyes to critique the book, Pastor Klein lined up some of his associates to read it. They, along with some of my former brother pastors, plus some pastors I knew from outside the Lutheran faith, provided the polish needed for the text to shine. I am indebted to each of you, my brothers in Christ, and to you, Jon. Thank you, all.

My son Alex crafted the cover for my memoir. He knocked it out of the park. And he's done it again for me. Thank you, Alex, for your creativity.

Finally, regarding my daughter Erin's artwork, which graces the cover: I hope you agree it serves splendidly to set the tone for this book. Thank you, Erin, for allowing me to use your piece.

1

Why I wrote this book

At a young age, I recognized justice and truth were important to me. Regarding truth, by the time middle school rolled around, I had learned the hard way that lying brought me nothing but trouble, so I applied myself to being honest.

As for justice, my childhood lesson came from, of all places, The Beverly Hillbillies. Whenever the Hillbillies' misunderstanding of a Hollywood way of doing things led to one or the other party's agony, I hurt for the side that was misunderstood. When I saw unfairness, I longed to correct it. I was eleven when Martin Luther King Jr. and Bobby Kennedy were killed. My sense of the injustice of those murders was profound.

In my early twenties, I left my family's Roman Catholic church. My folks were diligent in having us in worship and education. I took it so seriously my grandmother commented that I should become a priest. Ah, but I fell in love with a girl who was not Catholic, and she and I decided to find a church together. We landed in our town's Missouri Synod Lutheran congregation.

Taking the pastor's class to join the church, I noted how he used Scripture to back up what he taught, and found his explanations never contradicted the Biblical passages. While he did not talk down the faiths of other church bodies, he clearly defined key teachings. This allowed me to decide for myself whether I agreed with Lutheranism.

A correct understanding of God's Word became vital to me.

Here is how committed I was to doctrine. In my first year of seminary, I told myself that if I were to be a minister I had to agree with every doctrine. If I encountered a teaching I was not sure was in accord with God's Word, I would have to give it especially thorough study, and if I concluded the LCMS were wrong I would have to leave seminary and ditch my goal of being a minister.

That was no small hurdle I placed before myself. I was in my thirties and married, with four young children. I'd given up a stable job with a good salary and prospect for growth, sold my house, and left the hometown I never dreamed of departing.

Through three years of classroom study and one year of vicarage, no doctrine tripped me up. Indeed, the longer I studied and the deeper I delved, the more I believed my church body was sound in what it taught and confessed. When I made my ordination vows on June 23, 1996, I did so with conviction. As a pastor—first in a dual parish in Iowa, then in a church in Michigan—my conviction deepened.

Entering seminary at age thirty-five, I hoped to achieve another goal, equally as important as becoming a minister. All my life I struggled with my gender identity. With no knowledge about it other than I was male and thus it was wrong for me to long to be female, I constantly repented and sought the Lord's strength to overcome it. Yet my victories were tiny and short-lived. I never could hold the conflict at bay for more than a few days at a time. The older I got, the more uphill became my battle.

I hoped seminary would provide the ultimate diversion. I imagined so occupying my mind with the study of the Bible that there would be no room for my daydreaming. I would crowd it out and replace it with holy thoughts and holy teachings. I enrolled at Concordia Theological Seminary in Fort Wayne, Indiana, beginning with summer Greek. I loved it! The study. The students. The atmosphere. I buckled down and worked hard.

One week. That's how long I was able to resist the longing to be female. I realized seminary would be no cure. As getting married had not been. As having kids had not been. As repenting and trying hard had not been.

I would continue to repent, to hate this thing in me, to daily drown this part of my old Adam. Despite my deep dive in the faith, I succeeded no better than before seminary. As the years elapsed, my struggle worsened.

In 2013, I was crushed with gender dysphoria. I had grown to hate myself. I could not look at myself in a mirror. I despised being a male and loathed wearing men's clothes. I longed to live as and be recognized as a woman.

I was constantly angry. Every internal conversation about how I might resolve my problem ended with "You hate being a man. You can't be a woman. Just kill yourself."

Hoping to learn coping skills, I enlisted a therapist; my goal to feel content being a man and remain in the ministry.

Talk therapy achieved nothing. My self-hatred deepened.

With my faithful wife Julie vowing to be with me whatever I needed to do to survive, I retired from the ministry in 2014. I thought leaving the ministry would soothe me. It did not. The fire in my brain continued to rage, and I was in a constant fight for survival. The only escapes I could see were death, insanity, or transitioning.

Life and logic won out in 2015, when I transitioned to living as a female to see if it would help. Existing as a female wasn't always a smooth path, but I felt significantly better. Even so, I resisted. Several times I tried to resume living as a male. Each time, the dysphoria reignited.

In 2016 I legally changed my name to Gina, and in 2017 I had three transitional surgeries. As I entered 2018 I had completed my transition to female, and was prepared to live as one the rest of my life.

During the five years of struggle, I experienced a similar challenge as in seminary, when I would only allow myself to be ordained if I were in full agreement with my church body. As I learned about my gender issues and transitioned, I would not allow myself to compromise any of my beliefs.

My constant prayer to the Lord was to keep me in faith toward Him in truth and purity. Everything I was doing seemed contrary to what I believe—and I was told as much by plenty of pastors, by members of the congregation from which I retired, and other Christians. Yet, with every step I took in transitioning, two unimaginable things happened.

First, I never wavered in my theology. Indeed, I found myself even more zealous for sound doctrine than on the day of my ordination.

Second, every time I was pushed, especially by those who condemned me for transitioning, and I sought the Lord's good and gracious will, begging Him to set me right if I were doing wrong, every time—every single time, without fail—I had a resolve to stand up, address the person who condemned me, and continue with my transition.

The twin ethic I valued as a kid never left. My commitment to truthfulness required that I speak openly about my gender issues when I retired from the ministry. I already had learned how little most people know about gender dysphoria and being transgender. As I made myself a student of these things, I also witnessed how often transgender persons were the victims of injustices.

Before going public, in 2013 and 2014 I spoke with twelve LCMS pastors. Not one of them knew what gender dysphoria was. In my memoir, *A Roller Coaster Through a Hurricane*, I documented what I experienced with the LCMS when I made known my gender dysphoria in 2015 and after I transitioned. I will not go into all of those details here, only covering what pertains to the topics of this book.

Since I blogged about what I was learning and experiencing, many people contacted me with their stories of struggle with gender identity, including members of LCMS congregations and of other church bodies. I found these Christians to be as serious as I in their desire to lead God-pleasing lives, yet utterly befuddled how to negotiate this rough terrain.

I also reached out to the transgender community. I became active with a local trans group. I participated in two dozen panel discussions, most at Indiana University. When Indiana lawmakers were weighing legislation regarding trans civil rights, I got involved.

As a trans woman, I fully identified with the transgender community in their fight for civil rights and respect as human beings. As a Christian with a practice of the faith seen by many as old-fashioned, I was often isolated from them.

I heard the stories of trans persons who had been Christians or were still trying to be. Some had been kicked out of their churches, told by their pastors that if they transitioned they would not be welcome. One of those was

Maddie (I use pseudonyms for all trans persons), who faithfully worshiped in her Greek Orthodox church. Before transitioning to female, she explained everything to her priest. As Maddie told me, he condemned her on the spot, despite not having studied the issue, and told her that she would not be welcomed if she transitioned. Maddie found a church that was accepting.

Others knew the score and simply walked away. I met married couple Drew and Ashley soon after Drew told Ashley of his gender dysphoria. Devout Roman Catholics and conservative in how they live, they feared how their priest would react. Drew has been slowly transitioning, going out to selective places as Nicole. At Christmas, they used the holiday to switch churches. As Nicole and Ashley, they attended an Episcopal church, where they were welcomed.

Many I've met were also rejected by their Christian parents and families, who condemned them as sinners without trying to learn anything about the issue. For these trans folks, the Lord was turned into a mean-spirited tyrant.

Some were already in accepting denominations, or found a church that was. Too many perceived the rejection by Christians to be God rejecting them, and they gave up on the Lord.

In Chapter Ten, I profile a number of Christians who live with gender conflict, or have transitioned, or are parents of a trans child. Their stories demonstrate that Christians, devout in the faith and regular folks in their communities, are sprinkled in congregations across the land.

What I saw across Christianity and the secular transgender community was a black-and-white picture. If you were transgender, many Christians deemed you a sinner and dismissed you. And if you were a trans person holding a faith seen as part of the Christian Right , the secular transgender community scorned you.

There was no room in either camp for trans Christians such as myself. And, I kept learning, as one after another found me online, I wasn't alone striving as a Christian while identifying as transgender.

Having completed my transition in late 2017, I entered the new year thinking I was ready to move forward as a trans woman, but I experienced a profound change. The very thing that had eluded me my entire life occurred:

I felt like a male. All sense of being female left me.

In my memoir, I wrote in detail what I surmised was the cause of my gender identity struggle—the disruption of my endocrine system while a fetus. Now, having reversed my sex hormones to levels appropriate to a female of my age, I was left feeling exclusively male.

It was as remarkable an event for me as for Israel to watch Moses part the Red Sea.

When my sense of feeling male persisted, I went public that I had resumed living as a male. This closed one door and re-opened another.

The secular trans community didn't know what to make of me. While plenty accepted me, many did not. Not wanting to be a problem among a group of folks who are striving to make their way in a challenging situation, I stepped away from the local group.

Because I was again identifying myself as a man, some in the LCMS now listened to me. I renewed a few relationships. With the transgender landscape vastly different from when I began revealing my secret in 2013—the main event that put transgender before the public, Caitlin Jenner's interview with Diane Sawyer, wasn't until April 2015—to all that I experienced with the Church, there now were more opportunities to talk about these things.

In 1990, when I told my pastor I wanted to become a minister, I said, "I cannot not be preaching the Gospel." Since 2013, I found myself feeling that I could not not teach about transgender issues with my fellow Christians. In 2018, I developed an educational presentation called *Transanswers*. Early in 2019, I published my memoir.

My goal is to instruct Christians about these issues, especially pastors and all in our churches who work with their members. For the truth to be known. For injustices to be reversed. For misunderstanding to be wiped out. For the benefit of all Christians.

Too many church bodies, and individual pastors, church workers, and Christians, have done and continue to do a disservice to transgender Christians. Knowledge is lacking in what it means to suffer gender dysphoria and all that can result from it, especially transitioning sexes. In the reports, articles, and suggestions for pastoral care I've read, I've wondered if any of the writers have ever talked with a transgender person or done any thorough study of the topic.

In these pages, I endeavor to provide helpful information and sound doctrine as I explain about gender dysphoria, discuss God's Word, and provide a path toward compassionate spiritual care for transgender Christians.

I am in a unique position. Because I've *been there and done that* both as a minister and a transgender person, my experience is vital in key areas. As a transgender woman, I received the long arm of the Law when I craved the sweetness of the Gospel. Only the faithfulness of the Paraclete, the Holy Spirit, can take credit for my not ditching Christ and the purity of His Word.

Having been a minister, my heart is with pastors and all in positions of service in the Church. With gender dysphoria and transgender persons, you've been presented with new, unusual things which, on the surface, according to your education and experience might seem cut and dried. You want to do right by the Lord, and you want to do right by the persons you serve. It is my desire to help you, to provide the assist you need so that you might, indeed, do right by the Lord and His people.

The book's title and subtitle declare my motivation. I've written in equal measure for the sake of transgender Christians and for the sake of the Church.

My prayer is that you find me faithful to the Word of God in all I write. My hope is that the Church would have a compassionate heart for a group of people who want to love the Lord, but whom, too often, are rejected by Christians.

2

First thoughts

They are not freaks.

They do not carry a germ by which you can be infected if you touch them, or if they breath on you.

They are not sexual deviants, or sexual predators, or pedophiles, or anything else of a sexual nature which many errantly pin on them.

They are not part of a movement. They haven't jumped on board because of a trend. Or because they want to be cool. Or because they are unhappy with their lives.

They are not suffering a sinful temptation.

They are children of Adam. They were born into his Original Sin. They have been plagued with a particular expression of the brokenness of the human body due to the Fall, just as every child of Adam is susceptible to congenital defects, inherited flaws, and maladies.

They are children of Adam adopted into the family of the heavenly Father. They are children of God.

They are those for whom Christ also died, for whom Christ also lives, who also live in Christ.

They believe in the Father, the Son, and the Holy Spirit into whom they have been baptized. They believe in Christ Jesus for the forgiveness of their sins, eternal life, and salvation from death, devil, and damnation.

They hate their sins of thought, word, and deed. They love Jesus for paying for their sins.

They are your brothers and sisters in Christ.

+ + +

Prejudice. Fear. Shortsightedness. Stubbornness. Judgmentalism.

Side taking. Finger pointing. Wall building.

Them versus us—as if our battle is not against the evil of this present age, but against those who are of the same flesh and blood as us.

These are some of the weaknesses common to humankind. These are some of the behaviors we employ in order to make our point, to put people down, to keep from getting to know those we don't understand.

And especially to keep them out.

Christians are not exempt.

We value Martin Luther's summary of Christians, that we are *simul justus et peccator*, because we readily see the second part in us, that we are sinners, and we love to be reminded of the first part, that we are saints—that by God's grace, freely given us because of the work of Jesus Christ, we are justified in His sight.

Yet, the sins to which we are prone can cause us to forget the truth. None of us is righteous by our own power. All of us came into the world dead in sin (Ephesians 2:5). We are only alive through a gift (Ephesians 2:8).

God the Father doesn't love this one or that more than He loves another. Jesus didn't atone only the sins of believers, but of the entire world (1 John 2:2).

Yet, when Christians are faced with an extreme situation, because they are still *peccator* they are liable to think they are loved by the Lord because they somehow are more loveable than *those* people.

Or, as one man said to me when admitting his sin of adultery: "At least I didn't murder anyone."

+ + +

Those in service to the Church—whatever the capacity: pastors, teachers, counselors, or any of the other many and various offices across the church bodies—are wise to remember what every Christian is to grasp, that each of us is the chief of sinners (1 Timothy 1:15) and, therefore, prone to any of the conditions above. That while they have learned the teachings of God's Word, this has not made them immune from these weaknesses.

There is a position worse than not understanding something. It is misunderstanding something. When we are aware of a topic and believe we have good information, we can convince ourselves we know all about the thing, even that we understand it. But if everything we know is built on stereotypes, limited information, and the confines of our particular worldview, odds are we lack a true comprehension of the matter.

Remember, the sun doesn't revolve around the earth. Obvious to us, now. At one time, not so much.

A conversation I had with a pastor is illustrative. I sat across from him, in my second year living as a transgender woman, anticipating in my third year to have transitioning surgeries. I explained everything I had learned about gender identity issues. I explained how I found my gender conflict to be the result of my hormones having been disrupted when I was a fetus. Thus, I had a physical ailment, and was addressing my malady as one would treat an illness or disease, seeking good physical and emotional health.

For his part, he dove deeply into Scripture, focusing on how the Lord created us male and female. I told him I was in theological agreement with what he said, but that everything he conveyed completely circumvented the underlying issue.

Finally, I asked him if he believed intersex conditions exist. He replied, "I don't know." I responded, "In their report on gender dysphoria, your own church body's Commission on Theology and Church Relations acknowledges intersex conditions. Do you disagree with them? Do intersex conditions exist?"

"Maybe."

After an afternoon of conversation, I left with the sense that he heard nothing. His mind was made up and remained cemented. He had decided gender conflict is solely a spiritual issue, to be addressed with confession and absolution, Holy Communion, and ongoing pastoral care.

He was kind to me. He was friendly. He expressed concern and displayed compassion. Yet, because I felt I had talked to a wall, all of his kindness and compassion bounced off me and fell to the floor.

I experienced similar conversations with pastor after pastor.

+ + +

Keep in mind the following things as you read this book.

I was a minister in the Lutheran Church—Missouri Synod (LCMS) for eighteen years, and I continue to profess the doctrine to which I vowed on my day of ordination.

I write as a Christian who was a pastor, from my experience as a transgender person, and from my desire to help church workers better minister to the Lord's people.

From conversing with transgender Christians in numerous denominations, I have found that many churches are aligned in their understanding of gender dysphoria and transgender persons. I am not fond of generalities, but one applies in this instance: Christianity can be divided between those who accept LGBTQ persons and those who do not.

Of course, no one church body or congregation is comprised of one-hundred percent like-minded persons. Church bodies that believe in the six-day creation might have pastors and members who accept the teachings of evolution. A church body might be officially pro-choice, but have pastors or members who are pro-life. Some Christians worship where they like the programs and music, but don't agree with all of the teachings.

There are church bodies where transgender is not accepted, but individual members are accepting, and there are places where trans persons are accepted, but individual members disapprove.

In every chapter, I strive to be faithful to the Lord—to write from my education, experience, and faith—providing information, theology, and practical help that can benefit pastors, those in the many areas of service to

Christians, lay persons, and congregations.

In no word, sentence, paragraph, chapter, or idea do I promote diminishing God's Word, or convincing any church body to loosen its doctrine, or accepting anything which does not comport with living as God-fearing disciples of Jesus Christ.

Whichever your church body or area of service, if you believed what you confessed on the day you began serving, I hope you still believe and practice it. Whatever your affiliation, I hope you can read so as to feel I am speaking to you.

3

The Gospel

The first thing to go is the Gospel.

When we find ourselves confounded by a sticky situation, especially when we have quantified the other's trouble as one of sinning, we are prone to say, "Yes, Jesus has paid for your sins, *but ...*"

+ + +

We love to point to the Pharisees and the yoke of laws with which they burdened others, yet Christians through the ages and across denominations have done the same thing. Purgatory came into being because Christians could not reckon themselves holy enough to be in the Lord's presence immediately upon death. Purgatory was just one more yoke placed upon our shoulders, another law to fulfill.

When I was in seminary, I was surprised to learn a word I knew and used, *pietist,* had its roots in seventeenth century Lutheranism, where personal piety—holy living—was stressed so much it shrouded the Gospel of Christ. Instead of focusing on the finished work of Christ, Christians were turned in on themselves, on their striving, on how well they were doing in living holy lives.

The pendulum had swung from head to heart, from doctrine to experience, from Christ to us—really, to more laws to fulfill in order to be worthy of the

Lord's love.

In the Church, the struggle is for the pendulum to rest upon the finished work of Christ, that salvation is by the Father's grace, given through faith in Christ, worked by the Holy Spirit (Ephesians 2:8-9). The pendulum never rests, as sinful humans always find themselves dickering with the Gospel, muddying it.

We can't seem to let the Gospel be pure. Just as our sinful nature causes us to curve in on ourselves and away from our neighbor, it does the same with Jesus Christ and the purity of the Gospel. We find ourselves saying, "Yes, Jesus has paid for your sins, but ..." As soon as this *but* is stuck out, the Gospel is lost.

The work of Jesus Christ is objective. Christ's work stands on its own, upon His merit. The Gospel is what it is because of what the Lord made it to be, not by what anyone believes about it.

In the parish, when I sensed a student struggled to grasp this, I held up a chair and said, "If you think that what you believe is what makes something what it is, then you'd better believe with all your heart this chair is a soft, squishy pillow, because in a moment it is going to crash into the side of your head." I then swung the chair, stopping well short of his head. Point made: the hard truth of the chair is inherent. We can't just believe it into something else.

What you or I believe about the Gospel does not affect it and can never change it. But what we do with it can certainly detract from it, and perhaps even steal it away from those who long for God's love.

+ + +

This chapter is as personal as it gets. It is personal because of what happened to me when I transitioned. And because the same keeps happening with transgender Christians. And because it hits at the heart of our standing as children of God and how we enjoy that privilege.

No theological arguments I make can illuminate this better than my own Christian experience—how I learned the beauty of the work of Christ and the objective nature of my justification in the Father's sight, how many sought to take it away from me, and how I was sustained in Christ when I walked through the valley of the shadow of death.

I grew up Roman Catholic. I listened to the priests' homilies and paid attention in religion classes. I was taught to make confession, do penance, pray to Mary and saints, say rosaries. Ten-year-old Greg took seriously Father Joe's admonition: "Make the sign of the cross and say the name of the holy family, and each time you will receive a few days off Purgatory." Young Greg wore out that ritual.

I cannot recall being taught that I was holy in God's sight for the sake of Jesus. Because I struggled with my gender and longed to be a girl, I was convinced I would be damned to hell. I didn't even stand a chance at Purgatory.

Attending a new church in my early twenties, I heard the pure Gospel. I was holy in the Father's sight despite my sins—and despite how I kept committing the same sins—because Jesus Christ had taken my sins into Himself (2 Corinthians 5:21) and paid for them.

And did I ever need the pure Gospel, because I kept on sinning. And I continued to wish I were a female. And no amount of repenting, absolution, communing with Christ in His Supper, or being in His Word took away my desire or even lessened it.

In seminary, I was taught that we Christians live in tension. My particular tension was to always revel in the full and free nature of the Gospel, while never using it as my excuse to do as I please regarding my gender conflict. As I learned the history of Lutheranism, and dead orthodoxy versus pietism, I was bent on being guilty of neither.

I learned that my standing before God the Father had nothing to do with me, but everything to do with my Lord Jesus, and everything to do with Jesus being given freely to me. As the hymn taught me, my hope is built on nothing less than Jesus' blood and righteousness. *Keep your focus on your Lord Jesus, Eilers, for He is the author and perfecter of your faith*, as Hebrews informed me. It was for the joy of saving me that He went to the cross, scorning its shame, and now sits at the right hand of the throne of God (Hebrews 12:2).

By His wounds, I am healed, as the Spirit had Isaiah pen centuries before

Christ was wounded for my healing (Isaiah 53:5). As Paul informed the Corinthians, God made Him who knew no sin to be sin for me, so that in Him I would be God's righteousness, and God was in Christ reconciling the world to Himself, not counting my sins against me (2 Corinthians 5:19).

None of this had anything to do with me, that is, with how many sins I continue to commit, or with my making sure I don't take one wrong step in life or I might be tossed from God's kingdom, or of my needing to make myself perfect in order to be a righteous child of God. Praise the Lord that He is faithful and just, that He loved me and gave His Son as the atoning sacrifice for my sins (1 John 4:10).

My favorite verse is John 3:17, where Jesus informs us the Father did not send Him into the world to condemn it, but to save it through Him.

My favorite word of John 3:16 is *whoever*, which teaches that God wants *all* people to be saved and come to a knowledge of the truth, that *no one* who believes is discarded.

In neither of those verses does one read, "*But*, He only saves those who get their act together."

I love the absolutes of Scripture. *All* have sinned and have fallen short of God's glory (Romans 3:23). *No one* does good, not even one person (Psalm 14:3, Romans 3:12). *No one* can say that Jesus is Lord except by the work of the Holy Spirit (1 Corinthians 12:3).

In John chapter six, the Savior says that *everyone* who looks to Him, who believes in Him, will have eternal life and will be resurrected to new life.

Matthew recorded the Lord's telling us that *whoever* confesses Him before others, He confesses before His Father in heaven (Matthew 10:32). Does that include Peter, the one who swore up and down he would not deny knowing Jesus, yet before the day was done did exactly that? Yes, even Peter.

Romans chapter eight begins with the marvelous truth that there is now—present tense—no condemnation for those who are in Christ Jesus (Romans 8:1). Does that include Paul, the one who, only words earlier, admitted he can't do the things he should do, and finds himself doing the things he shouldn't (Romans 7:19)? Yeah, even Paul.

Second Corinthians contains the beautiful blessing that if anyone is—present tense—in Christ that one is a new creation (2 Corinthians 5:17). Considering how the old creation, our sinful nature, constantly rears its ugly head in our lives, this is almost astounding.

That's the beauty of what the Lord has accomplished for us.

That's the beauty of what the Spirit has worked in us.

That's the beauty of the pure Gospel.

Where is the Law in all of this? There is no Law in the Gospel.

In the Christian, the Law first works as a curb, to keep us from sinning. When we sin, the Law works as a mirror, reflecting our sin to us that we might repent. Finally, the Law works as a guide, showing us the holy path on which the Lord would have us walk.

While we long to fulfill the Law, it doesn't save us. And it's not our primary motivator. The Gospel is our primary motivator. Love moves us to keep the Law. When we sin, Love forgives us and Love restores us. Love abides with us through thick and thin. God is Love. And Jesus Christ is God.

Back to Romans eight: nothing—another absolute—in creation will be able to separate us from the love of God which is in Jesus Christ (Romans 8:39, the close of a section that begins at verse 31, which I often used in funeral services). *Nothing*. How's that for a promise?! It matches up perfectly with John 3:16, and John 6:40, and every Gospel proclamation of Scripture.

We shall not ignore or discount the need to repent of our sins and strive in holy living. This is what love prompts in us and faith generates in us, to acknowledge our failings, to confess them, to be renewed and refreshed by the Holy Spirit, to motivate us to do better, to be obedient to the good and gracious will of the Lord.

Lest the Good News about Jesus Christ be muddied and obscured, however, it is essential we preserve the purity of the Gospel. The Gospel is not dependent upon the quality of our confession or how well we obey the commandments. It is one-hundred percent the saving work of Jesus.

+ + +

Trans women and trans men are capable of loving the Lord Jesus just as much as the most pious-appearing Christian woman or man is. The Holy Spirit is capable of living in them, too.

We know the Lord plays no favorites (Romans 2:11, Acts 10:34). We believe that each one of us is to confess we are the chief of sinners for whom Christ came into the world to save (1 Timothy 1:15). We agree with God's Word, that on our own none of us does what the Lord wills (Psalm 14:3, Romans 3:12), that we all enter this world as sinners (Psalm 51:5), that we were dead in sin (Ephesians 2:5), and it is by grace we have been saved (Ephesians 2:8).

Because nothing is as vital as one's salvation, nothing is more important than the proper distinction between Law and Gospel. Even more, nothing rises to the level of getting the Gospel right.

The Gospel was taken away from me by many pastors and Christian lay folks: "Yes, Jesus has paid for your sins, but ..." The Gospel is taken away from transgender Christian after transgender Christian.

"Transgender Christian" is not an oxymoron. If it is, so is "autistic Christian." And so is "diabetic Christian." And so is "every-trouble-known-to-human-beings Christian."

Where it concerns transgender persons, getting the Gospel right is dangerous business. It makes it possible for "those people" to be children of God.

+ + +

When you are sitting across from the person who has just informed you they experience gender dysphoria, or the person who has made the painstaking decision to transition, or the person who has already transitioned, will you let your discomfort with the matter cloud your view of the Gospel? Or will you recognize that even the most baffling, befuddling, impossible-to-put-into-neat-boxes situations in life are never too bewildering for the Lord?

Will you flee from what seems a chasm of confusion, or will you recognize there is no abyss so deep or so wide that cannot be crossed by God's love?

Will you give in to the temptation to paint the picture with the darkest stain, or will you recognize there is nothing the blood of Jesus cannot cover?

Will you perceive only a willful sinner, or will you recognize a child of God for whom Christ also died?

A proper understanding that God the Father reconciled the world to Himself in Christ, not counting people's sins against them, means that forgiveness has been won for all, that anyone can believe in Jesus, and that nothing in all of creation can separate the believer from the Father's love freely given through His Son.

4

Key terms

Following is a list of terms relevant in discussing transgender topics. Not all of them are used in this book.

Assigned sex at birth. The sex designation of a child at birth, typically determined by the child's external anatomy. Synonymous to biological sex, birth sex, natal sex, or sex.

Binary. Referring to the two primary biological sexes, male and female.

Biological sex. Refers to one's chromosomes, internal reproductive system, or external genitals.

Blending. Not all trans persons can pass (see **passing**), so they seek not to stand out by blending in with how they dress, speak, and act.

Bottom surgery. Common term for the surgery to align one's genitals with her or his gender identity. Properly known as gender confirmation surgery or gender affirmation surgery. Formerly known as sex reassignment surgery.

Cisgender. A person whose gender identity matches the sex he or she was assigned at birth.

Crossdressing. Almost exclusively refers to biological males dressing as females, who have not openly identified as transgender.

Dead name. Many trans persons consider their birth name dead. While it served at one time, the use of this name conjures the intense pain of a misidentified gender. It hurts deeply to hear it used.

Deadnaming. Using the birth name of a trans person, especially when the person has asked that it never be used.

Disorders of sex development. An umbrella term for conditions of the reproductive or sexual anatomies that do not strictly align with female or male.

Drag. Anyone dressing outlandishly to entertain or party, but most often gay men dressing as women.

Endocrine disrupting chemicals. Substances—especially chemicals, pharmaceuticals, and plasticizers—that adversely affect one's system of hormones.

Facial feminization surgery. Used by genetic males to achieve a more female appearance. Includes reshaping the nose, chin, cheeks, and jaw; brow shave; forehead lift; shaving the Adam's apple; lip enhancement; and hairline advancement.

Facial masculinization surgery. Used by genetic females to achieve a more male appearance. Includes forehead, cheek, and jaw augmentation; reshaping the nose and chin; and construction of an Adam's apple.

FTM. One assigned female at birth, who transitions to living as a male; a transgender man.

Gender. How we experience ourselves—male, female, fluid—irrespective of our biological sex.

Gender confirmation surgery. Surgery to align one's genitals with her or his gender identity. Also known as bottom surgery. Formerly known as sex reassignment surgery.

Gender dysphoria. The distress many experience when gender identity does not match sex identity.

Gender identity. How one experiences themselves, independent of their sexual attraction.

Gender identity disorder. Former term for the condition now called gender dysphoria.

Gender fluid. One whose gender experience varies. A gender fluid person might identify as queer or nonbinary.

Gender reassignment surgery. Term often incorrectly used for gender confirmation surgery. It is incorrect because one's gender identity is not changed by surgery.

Genderqueer. One who identifies as nonbinary or fluid, or one who rejects societal and cisgender heterosexual norms.

Gender questioning. Those still unsure of their gender identity.

Hormone replacement therapy (HRT). Cross sex hormone treatment used in transitioning. Biological males take estradiol (estrogen) and suppress testosterone. Biological females take testosterone.

Intersex. See **disorders of sex development**.

LGBTQ. Lesbian, Gay, Bisexual, Transgender, Queer/Questioning. Also seen as LGBTQ+ to recognize there are more categories of sex and gender identification.

Misgender. Referring to a transgender person with a word, especially a pronoun, of a gender with which they do not identify.

MTF. One assigned male at birth, who transitions to living as a female; a transgender woman.

Nonbinary. One who does not identify strictly as male or female. A nonbinary person might identify as fluid, queer, or questioning.

Passing. A trans person's ability to look and act as the gender with which they identify so as not to be noticed as trans.

Personal gender pronouns/preferred pronouns. Of equal importance to one's name, each trans person determines his/her/their personal pronoun and long to hear others use it when describing them.

Puberty blockers. Used by transgender youngsters to hold off puberty so their bodies do not develop secondary sex characteristics that do not match their gender identity.

Sex change. No longer used and offensive to transgender persons.

Sexual orientation. One's sexual attraction to others, independent of one's gender identity.

SOFFA. Significant Others, Family, Friends, Allies. The acronym describes those who are supportive.

They/them/their. When a non-specific pronoun is preferred, especially for those who do not identify exclusively as male or female.

Top surgery. For genetic females/transgender men, having breast reduction, a double mastectomy. For genetic males/transgender women, receiving breast augmentation/implants.

Trans. Short for transgender.

Transgender. A person whose gender identity does not match the sex they were assigned at birth.

Transgendered. Incorrect term for one's being transgender.

Transgenderism. Incorrect term for the topic of transgender.

Transgender man. A biological female identifying as male. Also known as a trans man.

Transgender woman. A biological male identifying as female. Also known as a trans woman.

Transitioning. The process of one's moving from living as the sex assigned at birth to that of their gender identity.

Transphobia. The fear or dislike for individuals who are transgender, or for all things transgender.

Transsexual. Largely replaced by transgender. More commonly used in Europe, it typically refers to those who have had transitional surgeries.

Tranny. Slang for transgender. Always offensive.

5

What is gender dysphoria?

Gender dysphoria is the medical term for the experience that one's gender identity and sex, or how one was biologically identified at birth, do not match, resulting in conflict.

Dysphoria comes from Greek, meaning *ill feelings*. For example, a person identified as male at birth, whose inner sense is female, comes to have ill feelings of having been assigned the male gender.

A person with gender dysphoria has intense and persistent feelings of identification with another gender, and a strong discomfort with one's own assigned gender. Gender dysphoric individuals might experience distress with their body, with being perceived and treated as their assigned gender, and with the expected role of their assigned gender.

To have proper footing in understanding gender dysphoric persons, it is key to keep separate gender identity and sex.

Gender identity is one's internal concept of self as male or female, or a blend of both or neither. It is how individuals perceive themselves. Sex (male or female) is most often based on external anatomy, as well as a person's chromosomes. For most people, their gender identity aligns with their sex biology. For a small percentage, it does not. The term for individuals whose gender identity and assigned sex match is *cisgender.* The term for individuals whose gender identity and assigned sex do not match is *transgender.*

Gender identity is also not the same thing as sexual orientation. To be transgender does not speak to one's sexual attraction, just as to be cisgender does not speak to one's sexual attraction. A cisgender man might be attracted to women, or to men, or to both. He might be heterosexual, gay, bisexual, asexual, or some other sexual orientation. A cisgender woman might be heterosexual, lesbian, bisexual, asexual, or some other sexual orientation. Likewise, the sexual orientation of a transgender person might fall into one of the above categories.

It is common to hear transgender persons state that from their first memories they didn't feel like their biological sex. Children as young as three, as soon as they understand gender differences, might articulate that they are not the boy or girl they are thought to be. In modern culture, because children are given more permission to express themselves, a parent today might find their child very vocal and relentless in their insistence. Today's parent is also more likely to be receptive and compassionate in their approach to a gender dysphoric child.

With increasing awareness of transgender issues and treatment of gender dysphoria, a transgender individual or parent of a transgender child today can find considerable information and resources, and—less so, but improving—access to medical and mental health professionals experienced with or knowledgeable in the field of transgender.

Generations prior, when the culture was much less forgiving of nonconforming gender expression, a child experiencing a mismatch of sex and gender dared not utter that feeling aloud. One who did faced ridicule or punishment. Transgender was not a topic for discussion, so those struggling with gender identity in years past could not give voice to what they were experiencing, had few resources for learning about it, and were hard-pressed to find a sympathetic ear let alone an informed professional.

Consequently, many who grew up decades ago were left confused, baffled, and isolated.

When a person has a tremendous internal conflict, no means to deal with it, and no one with whom to talk, the mental distress can be excruciating. These folks might not even have pinned down that their angst is gender conflict. A trans woman reports she never knew why she didn't feel right, why she was always depressed. When, in her forties, she ascertained she was transgender and sought professional help, the pieces came together to solve the puzzle. She soon began living as a female, and now, a few years into her transition, finally feels healthy.

Her experience is not unique. For many who grew up unable to address their gender dysphoria in childhood, the gender conflict did not heat up microwave-fast, but was a slow cooker. They found ways to assuage the pain of their dysphoria, and temper the oft-accompanying anguish and depression. For some, alcohol and drugs became the only accessible medicines. Many took solace in crossdressing—either in private, or stealthily in public. Crossdressing is more common among males with gender dysphoria. Loathe to tolerate femininity in males, society is more accepting of women adopting masculine attire and appearances, which allowed trans men (persons assigned female at birth, but identifying as male) some easing of discomfort.

Not all people whose gender identity and sex are misaligned experience gender dysphoria. However, many find that the incongruity of body and mind intensifies over time and, eventually, activities such as crossdressing, which previously helped mollify the distress, no longer suffice. The desire becomes stronger to be perceived as and live in the identifying gender role.

With this slow-cooker condition, dysphoria often erupts when these persons reach middle age, or even older. Medical science has not determined why. Theories abound.

One theory suggests these folks simply get worn out by fighting the conflict. It is not unlike any tough situation in life: the ordeal gets to be too much and it overtakes us. The gender struggle wears on these individuals until it wears them out.

Another theory proposes that the condition develops as does, say, a slow-growing tumor. It begins small, and might not even be a bother. These persons have always longed to be the opposite gender, but have been able to abide and live in the assigned role. As time goes by and one becomes further entrenched (physically and emotionally) in the assigned gender, the longing deepens. The burden of being one gender identity internally, and another externally, becomes overwhelming, and dysphoria erupts.

In some cases, the person exhibiting gender dysphoria isn't transgender, but has a psychological condition which manifests as gender identity conflict. Quality talk therapy can help identity situations where another cause—perhaps a childhood trauma—led an individual to experience gender conflict as a coping mechanism. Walt Heyer is a well-known ex-transgender person. After Walt's surgical and social transition, the true root of his gender issues was identified and his incongruity resolved. Nine years after living as a trans woman, he returned to living as a man. Rather than acknowledge that misdiagnosis was central to his experience—and his experience alone—he has instead used his platform to renounce all things transgender. Because he is a Christian, and denies transgender, he has the ear of many fellow believers.

Correctly identifying gender dysphoria can be challenging for the one suffering it. A therapist will almost always be engaged, first to understand what is happening and to cope, and secondly to assist with the framework should a person proceed with transitioning. Because gender conflict is a complex matter with far-reaching ramifications, thorough and honest talk therapy is vital for a proper assessment.

Historically, mental health professionals used the term *gender identity disorder* to diagnose transgender individuals experiencing gender dysphoria. In 2013, the American Psychiatric Association replaced Gender Identity Disorder with Gender Dysphoria in *The Diagnostic and Statistical Manual of Mental Disorders* (DSM-5). Gender dysphoria was found to better characterize the emotional distress a trans person might have over the incongruence between experienced gender and assigned gender.

Many transgender advocates regarded the change in the DSM-5 as a step toward removing stigma against transgender people, that use of the word *disorder* inaccurately indicated a lifelong mental health condition.

Revising the name of a condition is a common practice. In some circumstances, medical advances prompt a more accurate description. In other cases, a different name is adopted to foster dignity for the individuals with the condition. *Physically challenged* rather than *handicapped*. *Visually impaired* rather than *blind*.

For many transgender people, the idea that they have a disorder is a sensitive matter. While one can acknowledge the difficulty arising from a mismatch of brain and body, labeling an individual with a disorder gives the impression there is something wrong with them. That they are a flawed person. Because one's sense of identity is so deeply felt, and is a very real thing to the person experiencing it, to declare it a disorder comes across as invalidating that person's very existence. It is no wonder some trans women and trans men—as well as persons who identity as genderqueer or gender fluid—react strongly to the suggestion they have a disorder. A trans person might assert, "I was born this way. I've always been transgender. This is who I am."

Despite the name change, the condition remains a medically qualified one. When gender dysphoric persons address their condition by transitioning sexes, they typically go on hormone replacement therapy, reversing their testosterone and estrogen from levels which fit their biological sex to those of their gender identity. Thus, gender dysphoria remains in the *Diagnostic and Statistical Manual of Mental Disorders* for the sake of identifying and treating it, and, increasingly, for being covered by health insurance.

While it is validating for a suffering person to have a medical diagnosis and term to describe one's anguish, it is just as important that those without the condition have understanding and compassion regarding it. Persons with gender dysphoria daily endure a real and formidable struggle between their outward identity—both biological sex and how the world sees them—and inner identity—how they feel about themselves.

Don't get tripped up by the word *feel*. We are not talking about how one feels, as in happy or sad. This *feel* equates to one's health, as in "This migraine makes me feel I'm being stabbed in the head with an ice pick" and "Chemotherapy leaves me feeling drained of all energy."

When gender dysphoric persons say they don't feel right, that their sense of themselves does not match their physical body and how the world sees them, they are getting to the core of what it means for them to be human beings.

The mismatch of gender identity and biological sex causes pain which hurts as bad as a broken leg, anguish which distresses as deeply as clinical depression, and suffering as concrete as losing a loved one to death.

They have dysphoria. Ill feelings. Feelings so ill they might find it impossible to live with themselves.

6

What causes gender dysphoria?

The short answer is we've not isolated a precise cause.

While increasing attention is being given to the experiences of transgender persons and the condition of gender dysphoria, medical science still lags in studying the matter. In the meantime, Christians fall loosely within three main camps, driven primarily by the individual's attitude toward the condition.

Evangelicals are inclined to see gender struggle as a manifestation of the sinful nature. The desire to be the opposite sex is viewed no different than any intense desire to act out against the order God created. These Christians are inclined to view dysphoria as a mental condition.

A significant and growing number of Christians understand the condition as a physical malady, one that likely began during fetal development.

A third group—those practicing a less stringent view of Scripture, and with a more humanistic worldview—believe the cause behind an incongruence of gender identity and biological sex is irrelevant, and that gender nonconformity is simply a natural variation of human existence.

Based on my personal experience as a transgender person, my view of the fall of Adam and its resulting physical brokenness, as well as extensive study of the topic, I find it highly plausible that transgender has physiological roots, which will be the focus of this chapter.

The list of conditions, diseases, and physical abnormalities that are congenital (present from birth) is lengthy, and many of them can be linked to a specific cause. An inborn condition might be inherited (or genetic), or influenced by environmental factors, such as exposure in the womb to viruses, medications, or toxic chemicals.

Birth defects range from being visibly discernable (such as Down Syndrome) to internal (such as sickle cell disease). Some are detectable at birth (such as cleft lip), while others are discovered later (such as Huntington's disease).

The origin of some disorders is straightforward to establish and widely accepted. A genetic test can confirm cystic fibrosis. The Zika virus is known to cause microcephaly in infants born to infected mothers.

For other conditions, especially those rooted in environmental factors, pinpointing a specific cause can be less certain. In some cases, a condition might be reasonably attributed to a sole source, but for the most part the exact cause is speculative.

That environmental influences can profoundly affect a fetus is, however, irrefutable. Fetuses are immensely susceptible to pathogens and foreign substances, particularly during the first three months of pregnancy.

Take, for example, the medication Thalidomide, which was prescribed in the 1950s to alleviate morning sickness for pregnant women. When pregnant women taking the drug began giving birth to children with malformed limbs, a connection was made between the birth defect and the medication.

Fetal alcohol syndrome (FAS), which results from alcohol exposure during pregnancy, demonstrates how a substance can profoundly affect a developing baby. Those with FAS can have physical defects such as malformed skeletons, and brain and central nervous system problems such as poor motor skills and intellectual disabilities.

The link in these cases is obvious. Thalidomide interfered with the baby's development. Alcohol has been proven to have adverse effects on babies while in the womb. There is no argument that conditions such as these exist, and minimal to no debate over the causes.

Conditions with less clear-cut causes are subject to deliberation and divergent conclusions. Autism, a complex condition encompassing a wide spectrum, has not been attributed to any one cause. Research has suggested that a combination of genetic and environmental influences increase one's risk of developing autism, but a specific cause has not been identified. The lack of evidence even leads to controversy, as indicated by the vaccine debate. Regardless of the uncertainty about a cause, everyone acknowledges that autism is a legitimate condition.

Depression, though it affects a sizeable portion of the population, is equally elusive of a cause. There are numerous factors that can contribute to the disease, which is complicated further by the uniqueness of each individual's biology, genetics, and life experiences. Despite significant advances in neuroscience, much of the brain and how it works is still a mystery.

Incongruence of gender identity is similar to autism in that we are unable to determine a definitive cause, and similar to depression in that the condition is experienced internally, intensely, and uniquely.

Where the comparisons cease is that incongruence of gender identity and the resulting condition of gender dysphoria are denied by many in society, and even more so in Christianity. Given the generation or so that elapsed between the medical profession shedding light on the physiological aspect of depression and widespread societal acceptance of the condition, transgender has a long way to go. Considering the discomfort many people have around gender issues, the road to awareness is especially long and steep.

What might be the biological basis for transgender? While the studies that have been conducted on the subject are limited, they tend to focus on two primary possibilities. First, that there is a genetic element, possibly involving multiple genes and polymorphisms. Second, that the hormones in the womb triggering development of sex and gender might have been disrupted or are otherwise not adequately functioning.

In the grand scheme of genetics and its impact on diseases and conditions, we've only just uncovered the tip of the iceberg. When it comes to transgender-specific links, even less is known, and no significant genome-wide studies have been undertaken.

We do, however, have considerable research to draw upon regarding the role hormones play in the development of sex and gender.

Sex is determined at conception according to the genes a person inherits from one's parents. Humans have twenty-three pairs of chromosomes, one pair of which is the sex chromosomes. Females typically have two Xs, males typically an X and a Y. A child receiving two Xs will be expected to develop female; a child with one X and one Y will be expected to develop male.

All individuals, whether they possess XX, XY, or an atypical chromosomal combination, start their development at the same place. The gonads of a fetus are undifferentiated until around the six- to seven-week mark. At that point, a gene associated with the Y chromosome, SRY, begins to trigger the development of testes. At around nine weeks, the testes release the hormone testosterone, which bathes the fetus and is responsible for the masculinization of the brain and genitalia. In the absence of testosterone, as in the case of an XX fetus, female genitalia will develop.

It is the disruption of this critical balance and timetable of hormones that many scientists believe can interfere with the gender formation of the brain. If, for example, a male fetus receives an inadequate supply of testosterone, or is exposed to an excess amount of estrogen, the result is the brain fails to properly masculinize and instead is inclined toward a female identity.

Inadequate hormone baths might be due to a genetic issue, to a fetus having malfunctioning hormone receptors, to a condition of the mother, or, increasingly, to substances known as endocrine disrupting chemicals (EDCs).

Endocrine disruptors abound in our environment. While there are some naturally occurring estrogenic substances, such as soy (classified as a phytoestrogen), most are sourced in chemicals, pharmaceuticals, and plasticizers.

Some common ones are

- parabens and phthalates, which are prevalent in beauty products and fragrances
- xenoestrogens, which are chemicals that mimic the hormone estrogen. An example is Bisphenol A (BPA), a chemical found in plastic and no longer allowed for use in baby bottles and cups
- dioxins, which form during many industrial processes

- perchlorates (a component of rocket fuel), fire retardants (applied to most household furnishings), perfluorinated chemicals or PFCs (used to make non-stick cookware), and pesticides.

Substances such as these can build up and persist in the human body, and are suspected to cause adverse health effects in addition to potentially intruding on the endocrine system of adults, children, and developing fetuses.

It is difficult to attribute an endocrine disruption to one particular EDC, and studying the cumulative effect of multiple EDCs in the human system is an extensive and expensive enterprise. Consequently, concrete evidence is lacking tying EDCs to the cause of transgender, but we have one telling study that indicated a correlation between a hormonal medication and a higher incidence of transgender.

Diethylstilbestrol (DES) was prescribed for pregnant women from 1940 to 1971. DES is a synthetic form of the female hormone estrogen, and at the time prescribed was thought to help women prone to miscarrying bring their babies to term.

Because DES was found to cause a rare form of cervical cancer in the daughters born to women who took DES, its use in pregnant women was discontinued. Since then, numerous studies have been conducted with the children (known as DES daughters and DES sons) whose mothers took DES. Health problems linked to or suspected from DES include, among many, increased cancer risk, reproductive tract abnormalities, pregnancy complications, infertility, and autoimmune disorders.

The potential of DES to have impacted fetal hormone baths is evidenced by a study published in 2005 by Scott Kerlin, titled *Prenatal Exposure to Diethylstilbestrol (DES) in Males and Gender-related Disorders: Results From a 5-Year Study* (available online). In the study of approximately five hundred DES sons, nearly half reported some level of gender dysphoria or identifying as transgender. Given the estimate that transgender affects fewer than six of every one thousand persons, the quantity of participants in this study reporting gender identity effects was striking.

Because of the crucial role hormones play during the development of a fetus, it is a reasonable possibility that one's biological sex and gender identity could be confounded by a disrupted endocrine system. Further and more in-depth study is essential to learning whether there is a connection and to what extent.

What about intersex conditions?

A subject that has received more thorough scientific study is intersex conditions, now referred to as Disorders of Sex Development (DSD), which warrant mention when discussing the topic of transgender.

DSD is an umbrella term used to describe conditions in which individuals are born with reproductive or sexual anatomies that don't fit neatly into those we define as female or male. In some cases, the condition is indicated at birth, due to anatomy that is visibly atypical. For example, a male baby might have a very small penis (micropenis) or a female baby might have a very large clitoris. Other conditions might not be noticeable at birth, but become apparent at puberty or in adulthood.

DSDs might have roots in genetic abnormalities, or might have hormone-disrupting causes. Let's look at a few conditions.

Androgen Insensitivity Syndrome (AIS)

AIS has three classifications—complete, partial, and mild—and it results in varying degrees of undermasculinization in XY (male) individuals.

Persons with complete AIS are resistant to androgens, or "masculinizing" hormones. As a result, the genitals do not form in the male pattern, and a person with AIS will have an outward female appearance. Because a woman with complete AIS has no uterus or cervix, the condition is often discovered when she does not begin to menstruate. Women with AIS almost always identify as female.

In partial AIS, there is a lesser extent of androgen insensitivity, often resulting in ambiguous genitalia, perhaps a protruding clitoris or micropenis. In mild AIS, the male has typically male genitalia, but less masculine attributes, such as lighter body hair and absence of an Adam's Apple.

Swyer Syndrome

Individuals with this condition have XY (male) chromosomes, but are born without functional gonads (sex glands). An individual with Swyer Syndrome appears outwardly female, has female genitalia but no ovaries, and will generally identity as female.

XX Male Syndrome

Individuals with XX Male Syndrome have XX (female) chromosomes. In most males with this condition, there is an SRY gene presenting on an X chromosome. SRY is typically only present on the Y chromosome, which results in masculinization. Men with this condition tend to have small testes and gynecomastia (enlarged breast tissue).

Klinefelter Syndrome

Most men have XY chromosomes, inheriting the X from their mother and the Y from their father. Individuals with Klinefelter Syndrome are XXY, having received an extra X chromosome. While most children with Klinefelter Syndrome grow to live as men, some identify as female.

Congenital Adrenal Hyperplasia (CAH)

CAH can cause intersex conditions in people with XX chromosomes. A genetic abnormality causes the adrenal glands to make high levels of virilizing hormones, which has a masculinizing effect. An XX fetus with CAH might have a large clitoris, or a clitoris that looks like a penis, or joined labia with a scrotum-like appearance.

Babies with ambiguous genitals are often subject to surgeries with the intent to "normalize" their anatomy. For example, a male infant with a notably small penis and divided scrotum might have his genitals reconstructed to appear female and thus assigning him a female gender. Many doctors convince anxious parents that this is the proper treatment, believing that doing so will make life easier for them and the child.

Advocates for individuals with DSD are striving to counter the stigma of the conditions and educate both medical professionals and parents to refrain from non-medically necessary—and ethically questionable—surgeries and treatments, until the child is old enough to make an informed decision. DSD advocates recommend a child be assigned a boy or girl gender after diagnostic tests have been completed (genetic, hormonal, and radiological) and the parents have consulted with medical professionals to determine which gender the child is likely to feel.

While some individuals born with DSD identify as transgender, most do not. Provided children are reared in the gender with which they will identify as they grow, gender dysphoria is not common among individuals with DSD. The two conditions—DSD and transgender—might both have roots in congenital causes, but it is important to remember they are distinct. DSD is a condition of sex development—affecting a person's anatomy. Transgender is a condition of gender development—affecting a person's internal sense.

Genetic abnormalities and maladies of the human reproductive and endocrine systems are numerous and commonplace. The Fall of Adam has led to disorder in all aspects of human existence, including in how humans form in the womb. Recognizing that we are all subject to the brokenness of sin can help us have compassion toward those whose physiology falls outside the norm.

7

What causes gender?

We often do not ask questions unless something unusual occurs. Most of us never wonder about gravity enough to look into why it keeps us stuck to the ground. Gravity is reliable. It's always there, doing its thing. However, if one day we found ourselves feeling half as light and able to leap three times farther, we would quickly dig deeply into the gravity of the situation.

So it is with gender identity.

Because we are in a time when so many find their gender not matching their sex—a situation which is not a respecter of persons, but is found across the spectrum of humans, equally affecting Christians who believe the Lord created us male and female, intending our self-identity to match our biological one—we do not have the luxury of assuming answers. Thus, because the Church cares for all people, and is concerned for the whole person, it is wise for us to dig into what causes gender.

So, let us ask: what causes gender? That is, when we consider God's Word, and that He created us male and female, and that His will was for males to feel like men, and females to feel like women, what is it that makes a person feel like their biological sex?

Is gender spiritual?

That is to ask, is gender an intangible thing, something God created so that we identify with our genitals, and so that we are attracted to those of the opposite sex, that we might go forth and multiply? If we were to determine that gender is spiritual, we could then find that any living in variation from strict male/female would be sinning.

Should the Church consider gender identity a gift of God, yet unknowable in how it works? Is it possible that gender works by the power of God's Word, akin to how Lutherans apprehend Christ's presence in the bread and wine of His Supper, and you can appreciate it, believe in it, and receive the benefits of it, but you can't dissect it in order to examine it?

Or can we locate a physical reason for what causes us to feel male or female? Is it scientifically knowable? Visible? Provable?

Is gender just as much a physical aspect of our being as our biological sex? Are they two parts of us which the Lord intended to complement each other?

After I revealed my gender dysphoria, I began asking people about gender. Assuming none of those whom I asked also struggled with their gender identity, I asked women if they felt like women and men if they felt like men.

The answers I received were intriguing. The first person I asked, a woman, answered immediately and unequivocally, "Yes, I feel like a woman. Completely." I thought, "Well, this is going to be easy." I could not have been more wrong.

Soon, I heard, "What does it mean to feel like a man or a woman?" "I am who I am. I don't know that I can tell you I feel like a man." "Gender is a construct. We learn how to feel from society."

Yes, there were plenty of straightforward answers, as with the first woman, but there were a confounding number of replies that prompted even more questions. And there were no definable groups, as in Christians answering as the first woman and the other replies coming from the rest.

Is gender a product of nature or nurture?

Do we feel and act and identify as either masculine or feminine by our biology, our DNA? Do we come out of the womb with it? Or do we learn it? Does it come to us based on how our parents, and siblings, and others treat us in those important formative years?

If gender is attributed solely to nurture, then can it be altered with a change in nurturing? Can we teach gender, as we are taught manners? Can we learn gender, as we learn math?

If gender is attributed solely to nature—if it is just as physical an attribute as our arms and legs—is it fixed? Can it be manipulated, corrected to what a person desires, especially for the one who suffers from gender dysphoria and wants to be able to identify with his physical appearance?

If gender is a spiritual thing—a gift from God akin to faith in Him—is any confusion of genders in the same category as unbelief? If so, what does that mean for the person who confesses, "Jesus is Lord," who experiences gender dysphoria?

I view gender as a gift of God, that He intended our sex and gender identities to match, and that gender is a physical thing. While nurture plays a role in how we develop, I find that development to be located in our personalities, our values, our work ethic, and the like, not our gender identity. Indeed, one finds just as many personality types among transgender individuals as among cisgender persons.

I do not agree that gender is a construct of society. Simply watch children at play. With no instruction, one observes play so typical of gender that we reflexively respond with stereotypical statements such as "Boys will be boys."

Quite the opposite of a construct, I find that gender roles have fallen in line with how the Lord created us. Where those roles have been ingrained to the point of unfairly limiting people—such as when men are unfairly promoted over women to positions of leadership—I locate the problem in our sinful nature.

Is gender genetic?

If gender is solely genetic, what of women who have Swyer syndrome? These people have female genitals and female-shaped bodies, yet they have male XY chromosomes. Or women with Complete Androgen Insensitivity Syndrome, who have XY chromosomes but female characteristics? The majority of people with these conditions identify as female. If gender is solely genetic, shouldn't they experience themselves as male?

Is gender hormonal?

I have male chromosomes. Before I transitioned to live as a transgender woman, my testosterone and estrogen levels were typical for a male in his fifties. When I went on cross sex hormones, I experienced wild swings in how I experienced myself. Four years after beginning cross sex hormones, I finished my transitional surgeries.

Shortly after concluding my transition, I ceased to feel female. When my sense of being a male stuck, I resumed living as a man. I continue weekly injections of estrogen. I produce little testosterone; "negligible," according to my endocrinologist. My two sex hormone levels reflect those of a woman my age, yet I feel completely male.

If gender were solely hormonal, it would seem simply administering testosterone to a man would make him feel more "male" and giving estrogen to a woman would make her feel more "female." Yet, we know this is not the case. In reality, the interplay between hormones and the human body is incredibly complex.

There is a broad range of symptoms resulting from hormone levels being out of balance, but sense of gender isn't typically one of them. If one's endocrine system had been disrupted prenatally, however, affecting the development of neural circuitry, a "normal" level of hormones might not be suitable. Indeed, many with gender dysphoria report a calming effect from receiving cross sex hormone therapy.

Is gender a choice?

You don't have to tell a cisgender male that he's a boy, or a cisgender female that she's a girl.

Whether people say their gender matches their sex, or that there is a mismatch of these, all say that their sense of gender was not a matter of decision, but simply one of recognition.

For cisgender persons, the question virtually never gets asked. As with gravity, it's so common and reliable for gender and sex to match that there is no need to ponder the issue. The gender-governing factors of fetal development—genetics, hormones—converge at the proper time and in the proper quantity to give cisgender people a sense of gender that aligns with their sex.

For transgender persons, it is a constant query, a lifelong process of recognizing one's internal sense of gender and grappling with the pain and difficulty of it not matching their sex.

If the Church is going to minister to gender dysphoric and transgender persons, the question of gender must be seriously evaluated. When the Christian response is a curt, "God made us male and female, period," we've denied that brokenness has permeated all aspects of our human existence, affecting not only the parts of our bodies we're comfortable talking about, but also our sex and gender.

If the Church tells gender dysphoric people to just deal with their thorn in the flesh and carry their cross, and dismisses as sinners those who have transitioned, we've denied that their plight is a physical affliction, as real and distressing as any other life-threatening condition.

If the Church has no interest in understanding what is behind gender dysphoria, or in listening closely to those Christians who suffer it, we've denied that we are called to minister to the least of these.

8

Transitioning

Transitioning is the process of changing one's gender presentation and role from the gender assigned at birth to the gender with which one identifies internally.

Transitioning is simple in concept and complex in practice. Methods and perspectives regarding the process have changed over the years.

Decades ago, transitioning was a secret undertaking. Individuals were encouraged to cut all ties, scrub their past, and move to a new town to begin a new life. While this might have been done in part to sidestep scandal, the primary motivating factor was to live without discrimination or fear of physical safety. The thought at the time was that the benefit of safety outweighed the loss of family, familiarity, and any potential built-in support network.

Today, transgender individuals transition in place. While safety and society are still overwhelming issues for many, few find it necessary to move away and start a new life.

There is no one way to transition. There is no one way to be transgender. It is said: when you've met one transgender person, you've met one transgender person. Because each transgender person's situation is unique—from the way they experience the inner conflict to their life circumstance—the way they approach transition can vary considerably.

Transitioning is multi-faceted, involving various aspects. There is a social aspect—altering how one presents oneself at home and in public, and using a name and pronouns that match the desired gender. There is a physical aspect—undergoing medical treatments that modify one's body and appearance. There is a legal aspect—changing one's name and updating identifying documents such as driver's licenses or birth certificates.

Many factors influence to what degree a transgender person will transition within those various aspects.

One person might only transition socially because she feels that is enough to ease her dysphoria, and chooses to make no significant physical changes. A second longs to go beyond social transition and avail herself of medical treatment, but is unable to afford it.

One person might choose every available medical treatment and surgery because he has the financial means or his insurance provides coverage. A second is unable to proceed with medical interventions due to health issues.

One person might make a full transition in all areas of her life. A second lives in her identified gender at home and with family, but not at work for fear of losing her job.

Regardless of how many and which steps a person might take in transitioning, there is a general order which is followed. Each step is utilized by genetic males and females in nearly equal proportion, with the only differences being in the medical aspects of transitioning.

Since transitioning for adults and children has significant differences, I address them separately. First, adults.

An adult experiencing gender conflict typically engages a therapist. First, he is seeking relief from his suffering. He might have already done some research and recognizes his condition as gender dysphoria. Second, if he plans to address his condition from any medical or legal perspective, he needs to be under professional care.

Therapists are often called gatekeepers. Without the endorsement of a licensed therapist, many of the steps in transitioning (such as HRT, surgeries, and legal name changes) will not happen. Because of the serious—and in some cases irreversible—nature of certain treatments, there are stringent protocols in place regarding transgender care.

Most health professionals and entities abide by the *World Professional Association for Transgender Health Standards of Care for the Health of Transsexual, Transgender and Non-Conforming People*. First published in 1979, the WPATH standards of care are based on scientific, professional, and medical consensus. The standards have been revised over time. Most doctors and insurance companies require adherence to WPATH standards before providing and approving medical treatments.

Since WPATH guidelines can mean a person with gender dysphoria must undergo multiple visits with a therapist, which can be costly and time-consuming, before being allowed to proceed medically, some transgender people find frustrating the gatekeeper role of the therapist.

The step of counseling and the role of the therapist are vital. Even when it seems an obvious case of gender dysphoria, there is significant value to talk therapy. Often a gender dysphoric individual is coming to terms with a lifetime of suppressed feelings. Some transgender individuals, as a coping mechanism for gender dysphoria, have substance abuse issues. It is important also to address conflicts in interpersonal relationships—those which might have existed for a long time, as well as any discord arising from the gender identity revelation.

Most of all, it is essential that the diagnosis be correct. While it is rare for gender dysphoria to affect someone who is not transgender, in some there might be deeper psychological issues that manifest as gender dysphoria. Ideally, a qualified therapist knowledgeable with gender dysphoria would thoroughly cover all ground to ensure an accurate diagnosis.

With an official gender dysphoria diagnosis, many transgender individuals will choose to receive hormone replacement therapy (HRT), either from a primary care physician or endocrinologist. While some opt to socially transition without having been prescribed HRT, many gender dysphoric persons desire the physical changes provided by HRT. The following is not all-inclusive, but speaks to the common effects of HRT.

For genetic males, HRT generally consists of estradiol, the female hormone estrogen, and spironolactone, a testosterone blocker. Finasteride might also be prescribed to further inhibit testosterone and enhance the effects of estrogen, as well as prevent and treat scalp hair loss.

Males report a calming effect from the estrogen and reduction in testosterone, which usually is the first indication their sex hormones are reversing. Physical changes begin after a couple of months and include breast growth, softening of skin, reduced body hair, and shifting of fat deposits. Reversing sex hormones does not change a male's voice or affect beard growth. The younger a person is, the quicker and more profound will be the changes.

For genetic females, HRT consists solely of taking testosterone. Reversing sex hormones causes increase in muscle mass, shifting of fat deposits, rougher skin, and thicker body hair. Full beard growth is common. Trans men might report feeling aggressive. The vocal cords usually thicken to cause a lower voice. Breasts do not decrease in size.

While sexual experience changes, genetic males do not necessarily become completely impotent nor genetic females unable to become pregnant. The effects of HRT vary among individuals, and are influenced by the person's age and health.

Trans men customarily welcome their beard growth, while trans women wish HRT meant their facial hair would disappear. Stubble and five o'clock shadow present a practical problem, and many trans women turn to permanent hair removal, which is expensive and painful. Laser hair removal is the quicker and more convenient option, but isn't effective for some hair colors. Those with gray, red, or really light hair must use electrolysis for permanent hair removal.

One's voice signals much about his or her gender. When a trans man's voice deepens, it is an important cue to being correctly gendered male. A trans woman who achieves everything else in creating a feminine appearance, but whose pitch is too deep, will often be misgendered male. Some trans women achieve a feminine pitch and manner on their own. Others employ professional voice training. Some have their vocal folds surgically reduced to raise the pitch.

Surgery is cost prohibitive for many. Increasing numbers of insurance companies include transitional surgeries in health care plans, but most still do not.

Most trans men desire breast reduction and elect a double mastectomy, commonly called top surgery. Until then, they bind their chest, an uncomfortable and painful practice.

Sex reassignment surgery, now known as gender confirmation surgery, or simply bottom surgery, is rare for trans men. The construction of male genitals can be done, but it falls short of achieving a natural look and performance. Trans women desiring female genitals have available a growing number of surgeons whose work provides both the appearance and function desired.

Trans women often need a tracheal shave to minimize an Adam's apple, and might get breast implants if breast growth is not sufficient from HRT. Because facial structure is different in males and females, some trans women opt for surgery to soften masculine facial structure, and trans men can have masculine features surgically enhanced.

Where access to surgery is highly variable among trans persons, the legal change of name is almost universal. While it is psychologically important to trans people to be called the name by which they identify, as a practical matter it is essential that legal and identifying documents also match. Some opt to have their birth certificate changed. For protection, a few will petition the court to have their records sealed. While it is now safer to transition in place, with most people involved knowing a person is transgender, this is not the case for all. Some still need to be stealth, that is, blend in with the world with no one aware they are transgender.

Regardless of which personal, legal, or medical steps are taken, virtually everyone proceeds with some degree of social transition. An individual might choose a new name, adopt a different hair style, and wear clothing more fitting to their gender identity.

This is especially true for young children, for whom nothing medically is done prior to adolescence. Diagnosing gender dysphoria in children can be a challenge, since they are less able to rationally describe their experience. It is not uncommon for toddler-aged children, at the time they are beginning to ascertain gender differences, to go through a phase in which they declare they are the other gender. In many cases this phase fades on its own as the child matures.

For children who are truly transgender, though, the declaration will continue and become stronger. The litmus test for parents and medical professionals is to take a PIC: Is the child persistent, insistent, and consistent in declaring their gender identity? If the answer is yes, and it is believed the child will benefit from being able to live in the expressed gender, the starting points are clothes, name, and socialization. If living as the gender in which these children experience themselves proves successful and sustained (many parents report a dramatic change from an angry, depressed child to a happy, carefree one), then puberty becomes a vital crossroads.

Males identifying as female will not want to grow too tall, develop Adam's apples, or have a deep voice. Females identifying as male will not want breast growth or menstruation, and generally will want to be larger in stature. These youths might take a puberty blocker, which keeps secondary sex characteristics at bay until they are certain they want the physical transition to accompany the social one.

When appropriate, transgender young people will go on HRT, which allows their bodies, having not yet gone through puberty, to develop in a way more aligned with the gender with which they identify. Trans girls won't grow facial hair, while trans boys will; trans boys won't grow breasts, while trans girls will; and so on.

Transitioning when young produces more effective outcomes for a person to live in a body matching her or his gender, particularly when puberty blockers are used to arrest unwanted secondary sex characteristics. Puberty blockers and HRT, however, are not without potential health risks. Because the practice of prescribing these drugs for treating transgender children and teenagers is relatively recent, little study is available to ascertain long-term effects. Indications point to a potential decrease in bone density as a side effect of puberty blockers (medically known as gonadotropin-releasing hormone agonists, or GnRHa). HRT might cause a higher risk for heart disease and diabetes, and estrogen, specifically, can increase susceptibility to blood clots.

Puberty is anxiety-ridden for any teen, let alone one struggling with gender identity. Add to that the standard adolescent mix of peer pressure, fear of being different, and trying to figure out where one fits in the world, and it's no wonder transgender pre-teens and teenagers are under a lot of stress.

The emotional and psychological benefits of a transgender child being treated with puberty blockers and HRT are significant, particularly since society has little tolerance for physical variances outside the gender binary norm. This makes the decision to use early medical intervention a very difficult one for parents, and one that should be made in consultation with a doctor.

+ + +

To the person who has not listened closely to someone with gender dysphoria, or endeavored an objective study of the topic, or attempted to walk empathetically in the shoes of a trans person, the notion that an individual would want to alter his or her body seems absurd.

To the person with gender dysphoria, who wants desperately to have wholeness of mind and body, the prospect of aligning one's physical self with one's internal self is curative. Just as anyone suffering a difficult medical condition seeks treatment for healing, so does the trans person pursue remedies that promise relief. Relief that, in many cases, is a matter of life and death.

The motivation behind an accurately-diagnosed gender dysphoric person's longing to transition must be kept front and center. Trans people have no desire to be trendy, or contrary, or self destructive, or unethical, or troublesome.

They just want to be on the outside who they feel themselves to be on the inside. They want to be productive, law-abiding citizens. They want to contribute to society. They want to be a part of their family. They want to spend time with their friends. They want to enjoy all the blessings of this world the Lord has given to us.

Really, they just want to live.

9

The suffering

Cisgender people possess a luxury they aren't even aware they have. They go about their day never thinking about how their bodies don't match who they are. They hear *ma'am* or *sir* and never consider how that greeting doesn't fit them. They pull an outfit out of their closet and never dread how wrong those clothes are going to feel on them. They interact with the public and never feel out of sorts at being perceived as male or female. They are free not to think about their gender.

For transgender people, and particularly those with gender dysphoria, the awareness that their internal sense of gender doesn't match their assigned gender is unrelentingly present. Furthermore, depending upon how distressful that incongruity is for them, they must continuously maneuver through a daily existence that does not feel right.

The suffering of gender dysphoric persons can be so intense that forty-one percent will attempt to take their lives.

That's two out of every five. Ten times the rate of the general population.

The struggle is twofold.

First, there is the internal strife—the conflict between a brain informing that you are one gender, and a body that is physically another.

It is hard for a cisgender person to imagine possessing the wrong genitals. Having breasts, where in his mind he has a flat chest. Having a deep voice, where she hears herself in a feminine pitch. And on it goes, in every aspect of a trans person's body and life.

When I was asked by a friend why it was so important to me to wear women's clothes, I replied to her, "Imagine that every day you were forced to wear your husband's clothes. And you had to cut your hair in a short, men's style. And never wear those dangling earrings, or paint your nails, or carry your purse. How would you feel?"

"I'd hate it."

"Because I don't experience myself as a male, I also hate it."

Most trans people report that from a young age they knew something was "different" about them. Most recount sensing they needed to keep it to themselves. There is considerable fear of the reaction of others which prevents many from disclosing their gender issues. Holding this weighty struggle inside is a considerable burden, and it becomes—gradually, methodically, constantly—harder to bear.

Even when one finally does divulge the struggle to another—an action itself fraught with tremendous complications—it is only the secret that has been freed. The internal hardship of the brain/body mismatch continues to be a massive obstacle.

Add to the inner conflict a host of external factors that make life immensely difficult for the transgender person. Although there can be a variety of reactions to the disclosing of one's gender conflict, often the person is met with disdain. Trans people face rejection on a regular basis—from the public, from service providers, from church, from co-workers, from friends, from family. They are excluded from holidays and other social events. They endure a much higher risk of being fired from a job or evicted from a home due to being trans. They suffer a greater degree of harassment and violence. Uncertainty regarding one's safety, one's financial well-being, and one's status with the people closest to them is a perpetual anguish.

+ + +

For too many trans folks, as soon as they open their mouths that they have this internal gender identity battle, their entire world crumbles.

It comes as no surprise that parents and spouses take the news the hardest. Of the many stories I have heard firsthand, rare is the occasion when both parents will at least listen and learn.

Too often, one or both parents simply reject the revelation. "You're not a woman." "I will never call you any name than the one I gave you." "You will not come to the birthday party dressed that way."

And the worst of all: "Pack your things. You're not welcome here."

That's heard by many teens and young adults, by significant others and spouses.

A rule of thumb regarding mates, whether married or not, is that at the gender conflict revelation half will end the relationship. Of those who hang on, if a first step is taken toward transitioning, another ten percent will leave. Eventually, if the transition progresses, only one in ten relationships will have survived.

Fear that telling someone about the conflict will be met with rejection drives the gender dysphoric person into himself, to suffer in silence. To try to cope. To live with this conflict indefinitely. To believe there is no way out.

The saying goes that suicide is a permanent solution to a temporary problem, but when you suffer gender conflict and have no one who will listen with compassion, death begins to take shape as the answer. The escape you seek. The relief for which you long. The end of your troubles.

This transcends generations. Children, teens, young adults, the middle aged, older folks—everyone longs for understanding, needs the compassion of loved ones, craves relief from suffering, wants healing and wholeness.

It's impossible to know how many succeed at bearing the burden of gender dysphoria without ever telling their secret. Understanding human nature, it would seem the number would be small. As I learned many years ago, we cannot not tell our story. The Lord made us social beings. We long to be connected. To share our lives. To be strengthened by those we love and who love us.

Especially when we are hurting. We need to talk. To get it out.

My church members would often pour out to me their troubles, many of which had no easy solution. Every time, they reported feeling better simply having talked it out.

By publicly telling my story, the stories of many were told to me. I learned the inside story of two suicides, one which dated to my youth in my hometown. A young man had hanged himself to death. That's all I ever knew. I now learned that, when he was found, he was dressed as a woman. This was the 1970s. Suicide, it seemed, was the only way he could tell his story.

I learned of another man who took his life. He had been arrested and, it would seem, feared his life would be closely examined. After his death, his family discovered the women's clothes he had hidden and the websites he regularly visited that told his story.

Whether with words or actions, we need to relieve the pressure that has built up.

In 2013, I told Julie my gender issues had erupted into dysphoria, and that I suffered suicidal thoughts. She witnessed me experience meltdown after meltdown, screaming from the pain and pounding my fists into the floor. She said, "I wish I could spend one day in your brain. I have no idea what it is to feel my brain doesn't match my body. I wish I knew what you are going through." Then, she got to work, asking questions, researching, finding me a qualified therapist.

Julie's compassionate approach—her desire to learn, her sitting with me through my meltdowns, her patience, her digging deeply into my plight—surely was key to my not despairing. To take nothing from the Holy Spirit holding on to me for dear life, always turning my face toward my Lord Jesus and His strength, if not for Julie enduring this with me I would have killed myself.

Too many do not have a spouse who will hang in there with them. Or parents and siblings. Or friends and acquaintances. Or bosses and co-workers. Or pastors and congregations.

I never wanted to tell another pastor about my gender conflict. I remember the day I did. I cried uncontrollably. I experienced the lightness that comes with unloading a burden.

I never wanted to tell Julie my gender issues had reached the level of dysphoria, that I hated myself, that I didn't think I'd survive if I didn't transition. I told her because I feared I was going to kill myself. I needed a way out, a way toward healing.

+ + +

This book focuses on transgender Christians, but it is vital to know that rejection is not only a problem among Christians (or those of other religions). I saw it across the board, virtually equal among those from religious families and marriages, to those who are completely secular.

The most intriguing was the following married couple. The wife was reared Christian, but had rejected the faith. The husband was brought up in a secular home. Both are politically liberal. The husband transitioned. The wife, who for any other issue would exclaim, "Tolerance and acceptance for all!" entirely rejected the idea of anyone being transgender.

She filed for divorce. Her spouse was devastated.

This is instructive. How can a liberal-minded person demand acceptance and equality, yet reject her own spouse? Christians and atheists alike can be brutally unfair in how they apply what they accept and reject.

Rejection knows no boundaries. Suffering cuts us all to the heart. Carves us up equally.

Gender dysphoric Christians long for loved ones to hear them, help them, hold fast to them. Too often the trans person is shunned for having simply disclosed a gender conflict, is denied any compassion for their agonizing condition, and is disowned for making the painstaking but life-saving decision to transition.

When you see a blind eye cast toward any number of harmful behaviors of others in the family—drunkenness, excessive gambling, extramarital affairs (the bad conduct with which we seem to be socially comfortable)—yet *you* are condemned for a condition you have no control over, it's hard not to call foul.

One Lutheran woman, whose son is transitioning to female, wrote to me, "I sometimes wonder if it would be more 'acceptable' in the church if my child were a drug addict."

When you see others in tough medical situations receive sympathy for their pain—understanding for the uncle diagnosed with Alzheimer's, kindness for the sister battling cancer, concern for the chronic pain sufferer who is now addicted to opioids (the physical ailments we seem to find agreeable to our sentiments)—yet *your* anguish is discredited as a "choice," it's hard to fathom the unfairness.

The suffering piles on. Gender dysphoric persons still have to deal with this harrowing mismatch of brain and body, yet in many cases they have to manage it on their own. Even if they never take a step toward transitioning, many will view them differently, treat them differently, give them the cold shoulder.

I simply announced that I had gender dysphoria and some of my oldest friends from church abandoned me—and I had stated that I was working to remain male. No matter; I had become an offense to them.

Trans people are regularly belittled and berated. Unfounded statements and vulgar insults are tossed around—both behind their back and to their face. "He's mentally ill." "I bet she was sexually abused as a child." "It's just a sinful temptation." "He thinks he's a woman! Ha!"

Even when folks have supporters—as I was blessed, having a faithful wife—the losses are tremendous. We might keep our spouse, or one parent, or some of our kids and siblings, but we lose others. Because we have caused division in the family—the topic of us becomes the scorned elephant in the room and the source of bitter arguments—we are now viewed as troublemakers.

Trans people experience a higher rate of unemployment. While increasing numbers of workplaces are inclusive, many trans people lose their jobs—some for simply indicating a desire to transition. Currently twenty-one states provide protections for transgender individuals in employment and housing. But, even in those states, the specter of losing one's source of income or being denied an apartment looms large.

Access to healthcare can be a huge barrier, and when trans people do seek care they are often met with discrimination and antipathy.

Fear for one's safety is a constant. When traveling or out in public, restrooms are always on the trans person's mind, and they experience much apprehension in trying to find a safe one. Facing the prospect of airport image screening and TSA pat-downs can be terrifying and humiliating. Simply walking down a street can bring harassing comments and bodily harm. Pointing and giggles are the least of concern, yet they hurt worse than sticks and stones.

I've painted the picture dire because too often it is this bad, and all the more so for trans Christians, in their families and churches.

Gender dysphoric and transgender persons did not ask for this miserable condition.

It found them.

They navigate a minefield every day. Internally. Externally.

The suffering is real. It is terrible. Often unbearable. 24/7/365.

These children of God will never need their churches more.

10

Your brothers and sisters in Christ

Through the blog I began in 2015, I have gotten to know many people touched by gender dysphoria. They fall into a variety of categories: some plan to transition, some are in the process of transitioning, some want to avoid transitioning, some have transitioned. I've also gotten to know many family members whose loved ones have gender dysphoria, with mothers, especially, reaching out to me.

Among these have been Christians, members of congregations across the spectrum of how the faith is believed and practiced. There have also been Jews, Muslims, and Buddhists. And there have been those who left the religion of their youth, those who practice new age spiritualism, those who are agnostic, and those who are atheist. Because I have written openly about having been a minister in the Lutheran Church—Missouri Synod, this has prompted a number of Christians to contact me who are members of LCMS congregations.

The purpose of this chapter is to demonstrate that the issues discussed in this book don't just happen in "other churches." Gender identity issues do not discriminate among congregations—churches large and small, urban and rural, liturgical and contemporary are all touched.

The Christians I introduce to you are a cross section of ages and situations in life. They vary in how they are addressing, or have addressed, their or their loved one's gender dysphoria.

Besides using fictitious names, to ensure they cannot be identified I have altered some minor information about their lives. The changes have no impact on the substance of their stories.

As of this writing, two of these folks are no longer members of their congregation. They wanted to remain in their professed church body, but after transitioning they were no longer welcome. Yet, they—as with all the rest—believe in God's Word, remain steadfast in their faith, and have no wish to change church teachings.

Meet Jeff and Susan

Jeff and Susan are lifelong Christians. Jeff contacted me in 2015, at his wits' end trying to live with gender dysphoria, which he experienced since a young child. He had told his wife, Susan, all he was suffering. While she was sympathetic regarding the suffering, she would hear none of Jeff's desire to try transitioning—living as a female—to see if it would give him peace.

These folks are in their forties. Their youngest was still in high school when Jeff and I began communicating. Jeff hoped to begin transitioning when the youngest was out of the house. Susan made clear that if Jeff transitioned she would divorce him.

Susan did not want to divorce Jeff. Jeff did not want to cause an end to his marriage. He undertook therapy, hoping to learn how to cope with the severe incongruity he experiences between his biological sex and gender identity. They have also seen a counselor together.

This couple is as traditional as it gets. Jeff's job is in a conservative field. You would never suspect anything unusual is simmering under the surface of what appears to be a regular guy and an idyllic marriage. Jeff and Susan enjoy each other's company, are active in the lives of their children, and worship every Sunday.

For now, Jeff muddles on. He wonders daily how he is going to survive. His angst, his frustration, his entire situation reads as if it were torn from a text book on the effects of gender dysphoria.

Meet Robert

Robert contacted me in 2016. Ten years younger than Jeff, Robert's profile reads almost the same—including employment in a conservative field—only with younger children.

Robert told me he does not want to transition. He is adamant transitioning is not an option, and that he needs to resist what he says is the "call of femininity."

Robert reached out to me because he had undertaken an unusual strategy he hoped would keep in check his sex and gender incongruence. He had heard of a man who was taking the same cross sex hormones genetic males take for transitioning, but for the purpose of remaining male. The man was taking one medicine to lessen his production of testosterone, and another to increase his level of estrogen, but this man was doing it *not* to transition.

The idea is that one might be experiencing gender incongruence because his sex hormones, while at typical levels for males his age, are not correct for his particular endocrine system. This is experimental; indeed, my own endocrinologist is skeptical that it is a viable therapy.

I liken it to using medication to alleviate depression. It often takes experimenting with the type of medicine and dosage to get relief, and these need to be monitored and changed over time. With hormone therapy, the tricky part is how much to block testosterone production and increase estrogen. While many gender dysphoric people report some calming effects of cross sex HRT, it is rarely sufficient to resolve the anguish.

After one year, Robert reported the HRT was helping. While his dysphoria was not fully alleviated, it was tempered enough that he could abide with it. After two years, Robert again stated he was doing well using HRT to soothe his sex and gender incongruity.

As it is common for medicines to create side effects, HRT comes with significant ones. For a male, most of them are fairly innocuous. Body hair (but not facial hair) grows more sparsely. Fat deposits shift, but because bone structure doesn't change this is less perceptible. Skin becomes softer.

One fairly noticeable consequence is breast growth, particularly for younger males. At first, Robert could get by with baggier shirts. Eventually, he bound his chest, a procedure used by female-to-male trans men to make their chests appear flatter until they can get their breasts removed. Binding is tight and painful. Robert told me he sometimes was left out of breath.

By the two year mark of taking HRT, Robert faced the need for breast removal. He admitted he preferred not to do that, yet, he was realistic; he could not live as a male with these breasts.

In 2018, he had a double mastectomy. He continued on his path striving to live as a male. He remains on a low dose of HRT.

Meet Carla

"Not everyone is 'happy' about transitioning. If it were possible for me not to transition and live my life peaceably being a grandfather to my grandchildren, I would jump at the opportunity to do so. I don't want to disrupt my relationships with my children and cause confusion to my grandchildren by my transition. Yet, I see no viable alternative to transitioning. I've come to realize that, before I started on the path to transitioning to live my life as a woman, I was slowly dying. I was living each day, waiting to die a natural death. I call this committing 'passive suicide'. There was no hope for me in this life. Now that I am on the path to transitioning to living as a woman, my life has gained new vitality, excitement, joy, hope, and peace."

The author of the above paragraph is Carla. As of 2018, Carla is her legal name, her birth name Carl having been replaced on her drivers license and other forms of I.D.

Carla was in her late sixties when she got in touch with me. We hit it off and began talking on the phone. We got to know each other very well.

Carla has adult children and young grandchildren. She's been divorced for many years. She was actively involved in her church, serving as an elder, a convention delegate, and a Stephen Minister.

In her fifties, she uprooted herself to live with her elderly parents, caring for them until their deaths. They belonged to a different denomination, so Carla joined. When I met Carla in 2017, she was still living publicly as a male and was in the process of becoming once again a member of a congregation in her previous church body.

She also had just started HRT, hoping it would provide her some relief of the torment caused by gender dysphoria.

This was not Carla's first time taking cross sex hormones. Her gender identity issues began in the 1950s, when she was a child. When Carla was a young man, the public only knew of one transsexual—Christine Jorgenson. Telling family and friends that your self identity does not match your biological sex was something you just didn't do.

In the 1990s, Carla experimented with HRT. She practiced crossdressing. She went out in public as a woman. She also experienced the guilt which goes with the territory. She felt she couldn't possibly pull this off, so she tamped it down, dedicating herself to bringing up her children as a divorced, single dad.

Gender incongruence doesn't fade away. At times, it rages in agony. At other times, it can be subdued. But it's always there. Typically, it worsens with age. Talk therapy provides minimal relief. Using only HRT to quell it, as Robert is doing, does not have a track record of success.

Serving children and parents, Carla coped. After her parents' deaths, Carla was once again living alone. Soon, she was depressed. She often could not get out of bed. She wished she were dead.

She sought a therapist, was endorsed to be prescribed HRT, and decided to try transitioning to see if it might bring her peace and healing.

By late 2017, Carla was living full time as a woman. It was providing the relief she needed. It can be treacherous to be in the world as a woman, yet have a man's photo and name on your driver's license, so Carla petitioned the court and had her name and gender marker changed.

One reason Carla and I hit it off is because she is as traditional and conservative as I. She holds biblical doctrine by the book. She loves the historic liturgy and hymnody. She strives to live a God-pleasing life. She takes seriously her standing as a child of God and a Christian in the world.

As Carl, she had told her story to her new pastor. He was adamantly against all talk of transitioning. They met numerous times. If Carla reported accurately, the conversations were mostly one-sided, with the pastor continually repeating every Scripture he believed answered all questions.

The pastor showed no interest in learning the science behind gender dysphoria. Carla recommended a book to him; he did not read it. He told her if she transitioned she would be excommunicated.

She began searching for another congregation, eventually resettling in the parish she had attended with her parents.

Does Carla see her transitioning as sin? "As a committed, born again Christian," she told me, "I did not see how I could transition without sinning in the eyes of God. I have since come to understand that this is not some sinful desire. I suffer from a physical malady. My gender dissonance is likely the result of something which went wrong in my brain development while in my mother's womb."

How Carla reckons the origins of her gender dysphoria, or "dissonance" as she accurately calls it, is common to those of us who take seriously understanding why we are the way we are—those of us who believe our physical maladies are the result of the fall of Adam, and not the simplistic notion espoused by some: "God made me this way. He doesn't make mistakes."

Carla humbles herself before the Lord, confessing that she is the chief of sinners who is cleansed by the blood of the Lord Jesus. She looks with joy toward the resurrection of the dead. She testifies that on that day Carl will be resurrected, will be made whole, and gender dissonance will be a thing of the past, never to come to mind, never to reappear.

Until then, she lives as a transgender woman, seen by many as sinning, rejected by the church body she still considers her doctrinal home.

Meet Michael

Michael is a genetic female who transitioned to living as a male as a young adult.

Michael's parents were surprised at their child's revelation, yet recognized the severity of the gender dysphoria and supported Michael's transition.

In their congregation there was a lot of conversation. The pastor was new to all of this. Despite not knowing what to make of it, he refrained from simply dismissing transitioning as sinful. Instead, he listened, learned, and leaned in with compassion. Michael and his parents remained members in good standing of the congregation.

Michael went to college, where he was able to blend in as a guy. While his gender was not questioned, his sexuality was. He was subjected to antagonistic anti-gay slurs.

As he persevered through four years of college, he saw no future for himself in his church, especially if he were to pursue a career in service to a congregation. Thankfully, he did not lose his Christian faith, as is the case of so many who are reviled by their fellow believers. Sadly, he left for a church where he was accepted.

Meet Justin

What do you do when your dad is a pastor, your father-in-law is a pastor, and you hold onto the doctrine you were taught, yet your gender dysphoria is crushing you so badly that you find yourself mired in a super-glue-filled pit?

This is Justin's situation. He found me through my blog. We began talking on the phone. For months, we talked nearly every week, his anguish always bleeding through the phone and into my heart.

Since kindergarten, Justin has felt he should be a girl. While he is able to identify as a male and be attracted to his wife, he longs to be the one bearing children.

He tries to distract himself. He pours himself into family and work. He goes to the Lord in prayer, seeking Christ's good and gracious will. He is considering trying HRT, to see if it might help ease his distress. However, he fears shifting his hormones could cause him to long more deeply to transition and live as a female.

Besides me, Justin hasn't revealed his secret to anyone but his wife, who has been as understanding as one could ask a spouse to be. I work to strengthen Justin, that he might find comfort, and in every conversation I proclaim the Gospel to him. I use God's Word, apply it to Justin, and remind him that the

Lord Jesus is his Lord Jesus.

Meet the Schmidts

This is the message from Anne Schmidt that greeted me: "Good morning. I would love to get your advice regarding my own child who is struggling with gender identity. Our home church will no longer allow my child in youth group. I feel I no longer have a church to call home."

If Anne accurately summarized what transpired with her pastor, Anne's child, who socially transitioned from female to male, is no longer allowed among his peers in church because his presence had become a problem.

Because of this, the Schmidts found themselves struggling even to attend worship, a wedge having been driven between them and their pastor. Anne and I have talked a number of times. She has studied gender dysphoria, that she might have informed conversations with her pastor. Thus far, she reports that the pastor refuses to listen objectively.

The Schmidts are devoted and conscientious Christians. All the others I introduced in this chapter are, too. None of them want to be troublemakers. All long, or longed, to continue to worship in congregations where they agree with what is believed, taught, and confessed.

They are representative of any man, woman, boy, or girl who sit in our pews, no matter how small or large the congregation, whether it is in a city or among the farm fields.

11

Theologically speaking

The Lord created man in His image. He created Adam from the earth. He brought Eve from Adam's side.

Male and female He created them. Genesis 1:27.

This verse typically is the first passage cited in the transgender discussion. It is trotted out in a manner which, when you're on the receiving end of it, tells you that's the end of the discussion. Sex and gender are black and white. Male and female. Move along folks, nothing else to see here.

Yet, we know this is not the end of the story. In Genesis chapter five, following the same "male and female He created them," we are told Adam brought forth a son in *his* image. The language is specific and deliberate. Where Adam was brought forth in God's holy, uncorrupted image, Adam's son was conceived and born in Adam's image—his Original Sin-tainted, fallen-and-fractured, death-bound image.

Where nothing bad or wrong would have befallen Adam had he obeyed the Lord, now everything bad and wrong sprang up, in the world and in the human body.

We are witnesses to it. We need only look around to see evil and the accumulation of all evils of the fallen creation since the first sin. The reality of our brokenness is substantiated in every natural disaster, every manner of entropy, every disease, every illness, every conflict, every pain, every sorrow.

No one who believes in the fall of Adam would deny that it resulted in real physical consequences. Indeed, from the womb people are plagued with multitudes of maladies—spina bifida, Down Syndrome, microcephaly, cleft lip, cerebral palsy. The afflictions accrue from there—diabetes, allergies, anxiety, glaucoma, arthritis, heart disease, leukemia.

Pastors, you know hard stuff well. All of you in positions of church leadership are all too aware. You deal with it regularly. You comfort and counsel the people who are under your care. When a member tells you she's learned she has multiple sclerosis, you respond with tenderness, sympathy, and compassion. You ask questions about the treatment options and what impact the disease is having. When a child of God tells you he has been diagnosed with bipolar disorder, you respond with tenderness, sympathy, and compassion. You take time to learn about the condition so you might provide wise and loving care. You strive to understand what the member is going through.

When gender dysphoric Christians open up to you, they will need you to respond with tenderness, sympathy, and compassion. They will need you to ask questions and take time to learn about this condition. They will need you to strive to understand what they are going through.

They will need you to recognize that they are suffering greatly. Gender dysphoria is for most a torturous, agonizing condition.

They will need you to recognize they are in a hard spot surrounded by a thousand rocks. There is no easy solution to this quandary.

And, above all else, they will need you to recognize they are children of God. Being afflicted with an arduous and perplexing condition doesn't change that they are covered by the grace of Jesus.

They long to love the Lord with all their heart, soul, and strength, and to enjoy Christ's gifts of forgiveness, life, and salvation. They don't want to disobey the Lord. They hate this cursed thing, this gender dysphoria, this befuddling, baffling manifestation of Adam's Original Sin. They are suffering and seeking comfort.

One's approach can either foster trust or drive hurting people away. Key to a compassionate response is refraining from simplistic judgments, including those that seem to provide, at face value, definitive scriptural answers. Let's round up the usual suspects.

Genesis 1:27. Male and female He created them. Simple enough, back in Eden. Today, very much muddled by a multitude of genetically- and hormonally-induced sex and gender variations. The Lord didn't intend disorders of sex development, nor dissonance of gender identity, but the reality of our fallen world means they exist. And, they might even exist in greater numbers, today, because of the endocrine disruptors discussed in Chapter Six.

People afflicted by such difficult conditions cannot go back into the womb and change their development, and spouting this verse to them cannot miraculously make the matter disappear.

What the verse says is fundamentally true. Expecting it to accomplish for the gender dysphoric person anything but hopelessness is a fallacy.

Deuteronomy 22:5 is cited next. "A woman must not wear men's clothing, nor a man wear women's clothing, for the Lord your God detests anyone who does this." (NIV)

Some call the passage natural law. If it is, it seems odd the Holy Spirit would plop down, among laws directed at Old Testament Israel, an edict meant for the New Testament Church.

Let's consider the verse in context. In Deuteronomy 22, God, through Moses, establishes for the people of Israel laws designed to keep order. The rules here go beyond just being a list of behaviors to do or not to do. Their objective is also to govern and impress the mindset behind the person obeying the rule. We are called to love and obey God, and to love our neighbor as our self. The intent behind the action is as important as the action itself.

Within Deuteronomy 22 are rules regarding separation: one must not sow two types of seeds in a vineyard, one must not wear cloth mixed with wool and linen. The roles of men and women in Hebrew society were clearly defined and segregated. It was unlawful to deceitfully trespass into another gender's role—whether it be a man attempting to avoid military service by dressing in female attire, or a woman pretending to be a man to enter the military, or a man dressing as a female in order to steal into a woman's space with the intent to commit adultery.

Aside from the fact that styles of dress range widely over generations and cultures, it is superficial to selectively lift this verse from a list of rules specific to Old Testament Israel and declare it a prohibition against current practice of dress. Does a woman wear pants because it makes her manlike, or is it a comfortable and practical choice of clothing? Does a man carry a "murse" today because he likes female-inspired accessories, or is it a convenient tool for transporting items? Does a man pierce his ears because he wants to look feminine, or is it a cultural expression?

The intent behind these adoptions of typically opposite-sex items of apparel is clearly not to deceive. Likewise, the intent of transgender persons in wearing clothes opposite their birth sex is not to deceive. Their goal, far from deception, is simply to alleviate the distress of their incongruity. To align their external appearance with their internal sense.

While Deuteronomy 22 was directed at Old Testament Israel, its underlying message still has application to us today. It is wrong to behave in a manner that is deceitful, contrary to God's Word, and contrary to the Golden Rule. It would be wrong to dress in the opposite sex's clothing for the purpose of harming another or for sexual gratification.

But this is not the intent of the person who is transgender. For people with gender dysphoria, donning the clothing of the gender with which they identify is palliative. It is akin to a person with depression taking an SSRI, or the person with rheumatoid arthritis receiving a cortisone injection.

Twisting the motive into something trivial—"He's just a dude in a dress"—or perverse—"He's out to abuse women and children"—or sinful—"He's just satisfying a sexual desire"—is not only an uninformed and unfair categorization, it is contrary to the Lord's command that we put the best construction on the matter, that we love our neighbors by giving them the benefit of the doubt.

1 Corinthians 6:18. "Flee from sexual immorality. All other sins a person commits are outside the body, but whoever sins sexually, sins against their own body." (NIV)

The Lord calls for sexual purity. This applies to all people: men, women, married people, unmarried people, cisgender people, and transgender people. It is immoral for a person to act illicitly for the purpose of sexual gratification (such as the Old Testament female-clad Israelite male sneaking into an unmarried woman's chamber to fornicate with her).

Gender dysphoria is not about sexual gratification. Recall from Chapter Five that gender identity and sex are two separate things. Sex is determined by anatomy, and generally develops according to a person's chromosomes. Gender identity is one's internal concept of self as male or female, and generally develops—assuming all goes as planned in the womb—in alignment with one's biology.

A person with gender dysphoria has an agonizing dissonance between body and brain. Those who take steps to alleviate this dissonance do not do so to satisfy some sexual depravity. They simply desire to be healthy and whole.

Matthew 10:38. "Whoever does not take up their cross and follow me is not worthy of me." (NIV)

"You need to bear your cross after Christ," is never prescribed to the one with cancer, or anorexia nervosa, or bipolar disorder, or a broken leg. Yet, it is often directed to gender dysphoric persons, by people who do not understand that the condition is just as real and physical—and as unwanted and dreaded—as any other arduous ailment.

Is "bear your cross" being applied correctly? Let's look at each of the places the Lord Jesus is quoted regarding this and see its context.

"And whoever does not carry their cross and follow me cannot be my disciple" (Luke 14:27, NIV), and Matthew 10:38, as stated above. The context: those who love family over Jesus are not worthy of being His disciple.

"Then Jesus said to his disciples, 'Whoever wants to be my disciple must deny themselves and take up their cross and follow me'" (Matthew 16:24, NIV), and "Then he called the crowd to him along with his disciples and said, 'Whoever wants to be my disciple must deny themselves and take up their cross and follow me'"(Mark 8:34, NIV). The context: He had just told of His coming crucifixion and resurrection, and Peter rebuked Him. After the admonition that they bear the cross, He proceeds to talk about one saving or losing his life.

The common theme is ultimately hating one's life in favor of loving the Lord, and losing one's life in Him in order to save it in Him. This is basic to being a child of God. It's First Commandment stuff, having no god before the true God. Trusting in Jesus Christ and not in oneself.

If gender dysphoria amounts to people loving themselves more than the Lord, then "bear your cross" is a proper admonition. If gender dysphoria is a physical ailment, as is autism and Alzheimer's and broken legs and asthma—if it's not a spiritual problem but a physical suffering—then "bear your cross" is not only the wrong admonition, it's just plain mean.

The gender dysphoric Christian longs for healing in the same way the cancer sufferer hungers to be healthy. Both know that earthly healing is temporary. Both trust that eternal healing will come in their resurrection from the dead.

Folks can go ahead and quote the above-mentioned Scriptures all day long. Gender dysphoric Christians will not disagree with God's Word.

When these verses are quoted as be-all-and-end-all "Thus says the Lord," the Christian on the receiving end is not helped. When the passages in question are cited, the gender dysphoric person hears, "Your situation is nothing more than a sinful temptation."

These Christians will find in their brothers and sisters in Christ those who don't truly understand, or are hard hearted, or simply want to be rid of this perplexing problem, or all three.

As I told pastors and fellow Christians of my gender dysphoria, it was clear those who had no room in their theology for one's being transgender could not get past the "God made them male and female" part. I heard it from every one of them. I sensed the crossing of the sex barrier was too big, too impossible, too alien.

Their advice was to remember my baptismal identity. Their counsel was to repent, to be cleansed, to be strengthened on Christ's means of grace, to bear my cross after Christ. I told them I did not deny my baptismal identity, that I knew I would be resurrected from the dead as a male, whole and freed from this malady, and that I bathed myself in Christ's means of grace through Sunday worship and daily devotion, yet my suffering continued to worsen. I begged them, "I'm either going to kill myself or lose my mind. What would you have me do?" The response from every one of them was, "I don't know."

The topics of transgender and gender dysphoria are inherently uncomfortable. Because we expect gender to exist solely within a binary parameter (indeed, male and female He created them), and because gender predominantly fits within that parameter, we're unprepared to deal with gender situations that fall outside our norm. We instinctively retreat, either by physically avoiding that which we find unpleasant or unusual, or by seeking an elementary means to explain it away.

Pastors are not immune. No one educated in God's Word and serving in the Church is immune.

I've known pastors who struggled with making hospital calls, finding it uncomfortable to interact with sick people. As I spoke with pastors about gender dysphoria and trans persons, discomfort in some of them was obvious.

Neither are congregations immune. It is easier to erect a theological barrier than open a church's arms to a peculiar situation or person.

It is undeniable that the Fall of Adam, and the resulting Original Sin inherited by all, has so corrupted humanity that even the purity of the male and female of God's creation has been affected. It is undeniable that our brokenness has so corrupted humanity that time and again we fail to love the Lord our God, and time and again we fail to love our neighbors as ourselves.

Praise the Lord Jesus for providing our way out through His death and resurrection, that through faith in Him we have the sure and certain hope of our own resurrection when we will be freed from every malady and made whole.

Praise the Lord that Jesus never fails to love us. He never fails to respond with tenderness, sympathy, and compassion.

12

What transgender is not

In my eighteen years as a parish pastor, I learned that even the best education cannot prepare pastors and other church workers for the situations that will be presented to them. Many are to be expected—marital discord, parent/child troubles, job losses, economic issues. Some require the softest of kid gloves—depression, schizophrenia, borderline personality disorder. Others are a punch to the chest—tragic deaths, terminal illnesses.

Plenty of situations are black and white—Scripture speaks directly to the underlying issue. A driver speeding recklessly down the interstate, a teenager defying his parents' curfew, a spouse cheating on a spouse, a woman gambling away the family's life savings. Such behaviors are clearly contrary to God's Word.

For numerous others, there is no clear answer. An elderly woman was facing an operation for which the doctor gave little hope of it being successful. The woman's four children were divided over what to do. Two wanted mom to have the surgery; two thought it best she not go through the trauma. I was called in for counsel. Is there a right answer in a situation such as this? Is there only one way for them to proceed?

In the sticky situation which is a Christian desiring to transition sexes, it is important to remember that it is not one of those black and white issues, and Scripture does not give us an easy answer. A proper understanding of what causes gender dysphoria is critical in taking both a Christ-centered and rational approach to the matter.

Through my conversations, I've found this lack of understanding prompts some to grasp at straws in attempting to portray gender dysphoria and transgender persons. Given the unfamiliarity and complexity of gender incongruity, it is not surprising that many are puzzled by it and susceptible to misconceptions. Let's dispel some of the myths and misunderstandings.

Transgender is not a mental illness

This is a common misconception by people who haven't taken the time to learn the reality behind transgender. Mental illness and gender dysphoria might share some parallels. Both are "intangible" conditions which primarily affect a person internally. Both can be exacerbated by external factors and failure to receive proper treatment.

For both, pinpointing an exact cause is difficult due to the challenges of studying the complex human brain. Mental illness is thought to have multiple causes that can overlap and increase one's susceptibility, including genetic, environmental, and biochemical concerns. Transgender is likely a product of atypical fetal development.

The anguish of gender incongruity, along with adverse external factors such as alienation, discrimination, and maltreatment, can have devastating emotional effects on a person. Some struggle for years not being able to put their finger on why they don't feel right. Some are aware of their condition, but for various reasons are not able to appropriately address or treat it. Some seek help and healing but are met with opposition at every turn.

It takes a tremendous amount of energy to navigate a transgender existence. One has to maneuver an exhausting amount of mental hacks to make it work. Recall back in Chapter Nine that cisgender people never have to think about their gender not matching their physical self. Transgender people have no choice in the matter—the mismatch is constantly present.

Living in incongruity is difficult and takes a toll. Consequently, many transgender people experience depression and anxiety disorders. It is essential that someone suffering gender dysphoria seek quality mental health care to help address the distress. Keep in mind, though, that the anguish (symptomatic) resulting from the condition and the gender incongruity (congenital) itself are two separate things. Brain gender wiring is formed in the womb. No amount of talk therapy, antidepressants, or "bear your cross" pep talks can change it later.

Transgender is not Dissociative Identity Disorder

Previously called Multiple Personality Disorder, DID is a condition where a person alternates between two or more distinct identities. The identities might have unique names, gestures, personalities, and characteristics, and they exercise control over the person's behavior. It is thought that DID develops in a person in response to trauma or abuse. Transgender persons are not being controlled by multiple identities. They have one identity, which happens to have a mismatch of internal gender and external biological sex.

Transgender is not a sexual fetish

Because crossing gender barriers is such a foreign concept to people who have never faced incongruity, and because many people have never met a transgender person, and because too few people make it past the hot button discourse to be accurately educated about the physiological reality behind gender dysphoria, a regrettable consequence is that some jump to a conclusion: transgender must be about sex. This idea has been perpetuated over the decades, led predominantly by a small group of sex therapists and psychologists focused on sexual issues.

If a person's life work hinges on analyzing sex, it is not surprising that person would find ways to incorporate a sexual motive into as many conditions and circumstances as possible. We all are aware that sex is a sexy topic on which to be fixated.

Decades ago, when our limited knowledge of the role hormones and chromosomes play in fetal development was even more limited, several misguided ideas were put forth to explain gender dysphoria. The focus was primarily on biological males desiring to be and/or take on female personas. If you can see how difficult it is in the present day for biological males with an internal female sense to step into a female role, imagine the obstacles that existed in the 1970s and '80s. Transgender persons had little recourse to alleviate their angst. Some took the desperate action of disappearing from the face of the earth, transitioning in secret, and reappearing with a brand new identity. Most, however, had to seek whatever solace they could. For many biological males with internal female genders, that meant crossdressing—either in secret at home or publicly in places they were unlikely to be identified.

Gender dysphoria researchers of a few generations ago, in interviewing small groups of gender dysphoric biological adult males, found some participants acknowledged they were sexually aroused by being dressed and made up as females. This led to the erroneous theory that men were drawn to crossdressing due to autogynephilia, which is defined as the tendency of a male to be sexually aroused at the thought of being female.

Considering extenuating circumstances is essential to understanding why sexual arousal might result for some crossdressing males.

The typical subject would be an adult transgender biological male, who had spent his entire life forced—through fear or life circumstances—to suppress the internal female sense. Beginning in childhood and throughout most of his decades, he had no outlet to express his internal gender, no terminology to even describe what he was experiencing. All he knew was he had to soldier on as a male in life, and sneak what little snippets of peace he could dressing as a female secretly. Couple a healthy dose of testosterone with the sheer elation one would feel at being momentarily free of the imprisonment of maleness, and it's not surprising arousal might result. For the vast majority of this generation of transgender crossdressers, once they are able to express their internal gender openly they no longer experience any sexual response. Regrettably, these obsolete studies and notions continue to surface.

The myth that transgender is a sexual issue has been bolstered by the historical portrayals of transgender individuals in TV shows and movies. Trans women especially have been hyper-sexualized on the screen, with producers fixating on males getting dressed in alluring female clothes, and applying heavy makeup. Just as inaccurate and damaging, trans characters were often cast in roles painting them as seductive and deceptive. Only recently are trans characters being portrayed on film as realistic, complex human beings.

Transgender is not a form of Body Identity Integrity Disorder (BIID)

BIID is an extremely rare condition where the sufferer has an intense desire for amputation of a limb, paralysis, or some other disability. The person suffering with BIID might feel, for example, that his right leg below the knee is foreign to his body, and he desires its removal.

Speculations on the cause of BIID range from psychiatric origins such as childhood trauma and obsessive-compulsiveness to neurological causes such as dysfunctions of the right parietal lobe in the brain, but very little study has been done. Many of the same sexologists who advanced the notion of autogynephilia in transgender people also set out to attach a sexual motive to BIID, although there is no reliable evidence tying the two.

Some have attempted to classify a gender dysphoric person's desire to have gender confirmation surgery (namely a trans woman having a vaginoplasty and a trans man having a double mastectomy) as BIID. This is a false concept. The person with gender dysphoria doesn't desire a body part be removed simply for the sake of having it gone. Rather, the goal is to correct the physical body to match one's gender.

Transgender is not like anorexia nervosa

One pastor asserted to me that telling a gender dysphoric person it is okay to transition sexes was like telling an anorexic person it is okay not to eat. The comparison: for the anorexic, not eating is giving in to the malady; for the gender dysphoric, transitioning is giving in to the malady.

I know of no pastors who would tell a person with anorexia it's okay not to eat—we all know it is life-threatening for an any person not to eat. I also know of no pastors who, if they had an anorexic member unable to eat enough to be healthy, would kick the person out of their church. Rather, every pastor would display sympathy and compassion, and encourage the struggling person to seek the treatment most likely to heal.

We now know the despair of gender incongruity is life-threatening for the gender dysphoric person. But, where our compassion rises to the forefront for other conditions, our discomfort with crossing gender boundaries takes precedence over encouraging the gender dysphoric person to seek the treatment likely to heal.

Here's the difference. For people who are not themselves anorexic, even though they might find it difficult to understand what would motivate a person not to eat, they are able to be sympathetic. Anorexia is a condition that is safe for people to acknowledge, and being in the presence of an anorexic person doesn't give them pause. Gender issues—pretty much anything falling outside our binary norm—give a lot of people the heebie jeebies. The idea of transitioning sexes hits our psyche like a deer caught in the headlights, and our instinct is to flee if we can, or put it in a box if we can't.

Transgender is not like kleptomania

A number of pastors have used with me the comparison of a kleptomaniac. With anorexia, the person harms self, but with stealing the person harms neighbor. I was told, "With a kleptomaniac, you would not prescribe stealing as the cure."

As with the anorexia comparison, the objective is to depict transgender people as weak in character, and to classify transitioning as a harmful behavior: the gender dysphoric person, in deciding to transition, is not only deliberately sabotaging himself, but is also damaging the well-being of others.

Let's be clear: the real harm—the original harm—was done to the transgender person back in the womb. Mitigating that fall-of-Adam harm, whether years or decades later, is the transgender person's attempt at survival.

The person who paints transitioning as a kleptomania-like sinful proclivity fails to acknowledge two things. One, that gender dysphoria is a serious physiological condition from which the sufferer seeks healing. Two, that a transgender person making the heart-wrenching decision to rescue his life and sanity by transitioning isn't stealing from others.

In the same manner that failing kidneys upend a person's life with dialysis and transplant waiting lists, or a landmine explosion upends a person's life with the loss of a limb, or a diagnosis of depression upends a person's life with multiple medication attempts and ongoing therapy sessions, many medical circumstances and the resulting treatments have significant impacts on not just the afflicted person but also those around them. We would not tell sufferers of the three above medical conditions to refrain from treatment because it is too hard on us. We would not equate their decisions with stealing.

If anything is stolen in these situations, it is that of which none of us are guaranteed in this complicated and unpredictable life: comfort and familiarity. It's easier to be on board with difficulty when the difficulty is socially acceptable and doesn't upset our notions of aesthetics.

Transgender is not homosexuality

Although we covered this in Chapter Five, it bears repeating because the two concepts—gender identity and sexual orientation—are easily confused when one is uninformed. Sexual orientation speaks to whom one is attracted. Gender identity speaks to one's internal sense of gender. It has been said that sexual orientation is who you go to bed *with*, while gender identity is who you go to bed *as*.

Transgender people are not drag queens

A drag queen is a male who, for purposes of entertainment, takes on the dress and persona of a female. (To a lesser extent, there are also females who perform as drag kings.) These folks are predominantly, but not always, gay men, and are often performers or attendees of nightclubs that cater to the craft. While some males who dress in drag might be transgender, the majority are content as males in their everyday lives. Drag queens dress as females to become, for a short time, someone they generally are not—the purpose is entertainment, not identity. Transgender people dress in their identified gender to become outwardly who they experience themselves to be on the inside.

Transgender is not cured by talk therapy

Gender dysphoria arising from one's being transgender is a physiological matter. It is not a spiritual weakness, nor is it a mental illness. While compassionate spiritual care and quality mental health care are essential to help ease the distress for Christians with gender dysphoria, those items alone are not known to successfully resolve the issue.

Trying to cure gender dysphoria with talk therapy as a spiritual or mental problem is akin to trying to cure cancer with talk therapy. In a tiny fraction of gender dysphoric persons, talk therapy might reveal a deeper concern—such as childhood trauma—from which gender conflict became a coping mechanism. For most people with gender dysphoria, talk therapy isn't sufficient to resolve their incongruity.

Taking to the extreme the idea that gender dysphoria is a spiritual and mental issue, some religious groups and licensed professionals promote the practice of conversion therapy. Conversion (or reparative) therapy is a practice in which gender dysphoric persons are subjected to psychological interventions in an attempt to modify their behavior and change how they think about themselves.

Despite clear evidence showing conversion therapy not only doesn't work, but also can have extremely harmful effects, some still engage in the practice. This has led to many states passing laws to ban the practice for minors.

+ + +

Without a good foundation, a building will be in peril. It begins with the cornerstone being properly laid on firm ground, a downright biblical truth.

So it goes with addressing the sticky situations which present themselves to those ministering in our churches.

We dare not jump to conclusions, as when hearing one side of an argument between a husband and wife. When one spouse presents the issue, it might sound open and shut that the other is guilty. Yet, when the other gets a chance to speak, information is brought to light that had been kept in the dark.

We dare not make hasty decisions based on incomplete or faulty information. We are wise to strive for facts over opinions, objective standards over subjective feelings.

Those listening to anyone experiencing gender incongruity while holding errant ideas will build their response upon a cornerstone set on sinking sand. The hurting Christian will pay the price, as will likely the person's family, as will possibly the entire congregation.

Providing care to a transgender person is as difficult a situation in which those serving Christians will find themselves. It is tempting to condemn and dismiss rather than put in the hard and time-consuming work to discern and understand. It is tempting to slap a false label on the perplexing matter and ship it away rather than sit down to read the technical manual it requires.

Considering some of the past situations through which Christianity, church bodies, and individual Christians have strained and strived will enlighten how we might better negotiate how to minister to transgender Christians.

13

Sticky situations

In many churches, the gender dysphoric person too often receives only a glimpse of sympathy: "I don't know what you're going through, but I can tell it is terrible, that you are hurting deeply." As long as there is no movement toward transitioning, the compassion remains. But, the moment the gender dysphoric person talks of transitioning, or wants to attend worship as the opposite sex, the narrative quickly becomes conditional.

Recall the folks I introduced to you in Chapter Ten. Every one of them wished they had the strength to find comfort in their birth sex. Carla strived for decades to abide as a male. Finally worn out by the suffering, she transitioned. Carla didn't want to have to transition, didn't want to hurt her family or anyone, didn't want to trade one struggle for another.

Carla's pastor had declared she would be excommunicated if she transitioned, so she made it easy on him: Carla showed herself the door and found a church where she was welcomed with dignity.

Translation: you can be a Christian, just do it somewhere else.

Carla had met numerous times with her pastor. She gave him materials to read. Based on these conversations, she believed he either only skimmed over them or didn't bother reading them at all. If she accurately relayed his attitude, his mind was made up, there was nothing to learn, and he was never going to budge from "male and female He created them" and transitioning is sinful.

Before I transitioned, I spoke with a number of pastors about my gender dysphoria. Finally at wit's end, I told one of them I was going to live as a female to see if it helped. His response? "I think it's time. You should do it."

That pastor agreed it was time to see if my suffering would be relieved by transitioning. He said nothing of my sinning should I do it. Julie and I were not attending his church, so he didn't have the practical matter of dealing with our presence. One of his members spoke with him about me. If she informed me correctly, he said we were welcome to attend worship, but we could not receive Holy Communion.

In a congregation Julie and I had joined, where the pastors were given an ultimatum—either we go or the church gets kicked out of the synod—we offered our resignation from membership to spare them more trouble. They continued to welcome us to worship—which we did for another nineteen months—but we could not commune. We were not called to repent, nor given a list of our sins, but we were treated as unrepentant sinners.

And, though we did not take them up on it, they offered to commune us in private.

Translation: Jesus' blood covers you, but not when others are watching.

Another pastor advised that Julie and I would be welcome to worship when I was living as a female, but we could not be members. If I wanted to attend Holy Communion, I would need to be dressed as a male.

Translation: it is your appearance, your presenting gender, that makes you worthy to receive the Lord Jesus' gifts.

It is easy to erect a wall between ourselves and the objects of our discomfort, conveniently classify them as worse sinners than the rest of us, place conditions on Jesus' love, and hope they take the hint and leave to become someone else's problem.

+ + +

Christianity overall, specific church bodies, ministers and counselors and leaders, and individual Christians have always found themselves in sticky situations. Plenty of times, they got the matter wrong. We remember how the Roman Church treated Galileo and the at-that-time heretical notion that the earth revolved around the sun.

Eventually, we learned the truth. Scientific discovery widened and deepened. The Word of God didn't change, but our understanding did. We recognized truths about the world and changed our minds.

In the previous chapter, I noted transgender should not be likened to anorexia or kleptomania. Few will find themselves ministering to one suffering kleptomania, where neighbor is harmed, or an anorexic person, where self is harmed. Many will, however, find themselves ministering to alcoholics, where both self and neighbor typically are harmed.

Scientific discovery has taught us much about alcoholism. I recall when viewing alcoholism as a disease gained acceptance, I personally found it absurd that those who drank too much were being given a *get out of bad behavior free* card. During my years of ministry, I got to know a number of alcoholics. Their testimony led me to study the matter.

In college, I learned this definition: education = changed behavior. With education and experience, I changed my mind regarding alcoholism.

No one, today, would declare unrepentant an alcoholic who longs to remain in recovery, but struggles to do so. A few generations ago, those who "fell off the wagon" were declared sinners and not welcome in church. Though the Word of God hasn't changed, education has led us to better understand the difficulties behind this sticky situation.

Until a generation or so ago, our view of depression was that depressed persons simply needed to try harder, to get their act together. Depressed Christians might be accused of sinning, that they were too focused on themselves, that they were not being thankful for all the Lord does, that they needed to have a stronger faith. We have learned a lot about this human condition, and we've changed our minds. The Word of God didn't change, but our attitudes have changed about this sticky situation.

If you are my age, you likely recall the introduction of heart transplants. My mother echoed what so many were saying: "They're playing God." With time and proper understanding about how we humans work, heart transplants were accepted. The Word of God didn't change, yet we changed our view, and heart transplants ceased to be a sticky situation for Christians.

For much of Christian history, those who committed suicide were thought to be eternally lost. Indeed, indicative of how delicate the topic remains, among the questions most asked of me as pastor was, "Do people who kill themselves go to hell?" We have learned a lot about the human condition. We have applied our theology better. Cultural changes also have affected our attitudes. The Word of God didn't change, but we changed our view about this sticky situation.

Until a US Supreme Court decision in 1967, interracial marriage could be illegal, and it was in many states across the nation. Many Christians viewed mixed race marriages as sinful. The marriage law changed, the civil rights movement fostered change, and now most Christians have changed their minds toward interracial marriage. The Word of God didn't change—indeed, the New Testament calls Christians not to be unequally yoked with unbelievers, but says nothing of people of mixed color, culture, or language being married—but we changed our view about this sticky situation.

As Christians strive to be in the world but not of the world, they are profoundly influenced by the world. The Word of God has not changed, but many church bodies have changed their stances on women having a voice in church matters, much of it gaining steam with the secular women's movement of the late 1960s.

It had been a no-no at one time to own life insurance. Doing so meant a Christian was not trusting the Lord. Though God's Word didn't change, purchasing life insurance became a widely accepted practice by Christians.

In these handful of examples, we see that Christians have changed their minds while reading the same Bible their forebears studied. Christians have changed their minds theologically, due to scientific discovery, as a result of man-made laws, by influence from culture, and with the passing of time.

For most of the history of the Christian Church, no one would have thought science would reveal what it has about the various maladies that affect us. In how transgender is currently viewed, I liken it to where depression was fifty years ago.

Might we humbly recognize we do not have all the answers regarding transgender? It's not even been a decade since we began talking openly about it. We are only at the beginning of learning *about* what it is and learning *from* those who experience it.

As we allow history to be our teacher, might we not also listen to our Christians who suffer in this stickiest of situations, that they trust Jesus as much as the next Christian but their faith cannot resolve their conflict any more than faith can cure cancer?

In these stickiest of situations, will you kick these hurting brothers and sisters in Christ when they need the Lord Jesus the most, or will you help them feel the healing hand of their Savior?

Will you only have words of condemnation and judgment for them, or will you guide the weary to where they'll find rest?

Will you stand by when others heap scorn and disparagement, or will you shine the light of the One who is merciful and gracious?

When we are in the hardest, worst, thorniest of life's situations, and we cry out for compassion and understanding in Christ's Church, which one wins—the long arm of the Law and condemnation, or the good news of the Gospel and compassion?

14

Spiritual care

Spiritual care begins in the attitude and actions of the one providing it. All in positions of ministry must be approachable, quick to listen, and slow to speak. These attributes are never more important than with gender dysphoric and transgender persons.

Spiritual care for gender dysphoric and transgender persons begins before they sit down with their pastor, Christian counselor, and the like. Indeed, they will not even approach anyone—they will not share this difficult information with anyone in authority—if they believe that person has a negative attitude towards trans persons, if they believe that person will only have words of judgment. Thus, especially, in what pastors preach, in what instructors teach, and in what is published in the church newsletter and on the website, on this topic, church leaders must be mindful who might be on the receiving end.

When trans Christians tell me of their experience, especially with pastors, one of the saddest things I hear is, "My pastor didn't show any interest in listening to me. As soon as I spoke about my situation, all I got was an earful."

Initial visit

Just as being diagnosed with a tumor does not automatically mean surgery and chemotherapy, experiencing gender dysphoria does not mean one will transition, or that one is transgender. Having informed yourself about these issues, you have a host of ways to help.

Begin with getting to know them. Let them talk. Facilitate the conversation by asking open-ended questions. Listen.

When did he begin to feel gender dissonance? How has she experienced it? What does he believe about himself?

The way trans people view themselves and how they communicate or explain that view can vary. An individual's characterization might also change over time. Early in the throes of gender dysphoria, they might be experiencing significant distress and emotion. As a result, they might at first be especially insistent in the declarations they make but, later, as they develop a deeper comprehension of themselves, their tone might become less insistent. Conversely, others might be hesitant and unsure in the beginning, but become more emphatic as time passes.

Reactions from family, friends, coworkers, and church members can also significantly influence the language and attitude they adopt. If those in whom trans persons confide are insensitive, unsympathetic, or even cruel, it is to be expected they would feel backed into a corner and compelled to assert their case more forcefully.

It is important to recognize statements for the motivation and underlying concerns behind them, and not contradict these folks or object to statements you find perplexing.

A trans woman (biological male identifying as female) might say "I am and have always been a woman." To someone who witnessed that individual presenting as male for years, this strikes as an odd declaration. Because one's internal identity is paramount in how one views oneself, what the trans woman means is she understands her core being from birth to be, and to have always been, female. Presenting as a male externally doesn't change the heart of her matter—that her sense of being female has existed in her for as long as she can remember.

The phrase, "A woman trapped in a man's body," is uttered often by non-trans persons in a flippant manner, but sometimes dysphoric individuals say this in their quest to find words to explain what is going on inside them. The implication is the same as in the previous paragraph: the individual's internal sense of herself is female.

For some, the gender identity conflict might not fall into the binary categories of male or female. People who classify themselves as genderqueer, gender questioning, or gender fluid, might tell you they cannot pin down an internal sense of gender, or perhaps they feel a sense of both male and female, or might even feel masculine one day but feminine the next. Some prefer the use of gender-neutral "they/them/their" as pronouns. As we recall from the chapters on gender, this feeling experienced by genderqueer persons of not being male or female, or of shifting between the two, is not a matter of choice, but an inherent internal sense.

Who else have these persons told of their gender conflict? How did they react?

You, to whom they have turned for spiritual care, might be the first person a gender dysphoric person confides in, or you might be the fiftieth. Regardless, telling this story is difficult. No matter the relationship or level of trust that heretofore existed between two people, opening up about a gender identity struggle is daunting.

While a trans person might be familiar with the recipient's general demeanor in the face of challenging situations, there is simply no predicting someone's reaction to this particular news. This puts trans persons in an extremely vulnerable position, on top of an already stressful state. When the courage is mustered to disclose a gender identity conflict, it can take a while for them to begin the conversation. With the topic at hand not only deeply complex, but also widely misconstrued, it can be tough to find the words. Some find it too intimidating to have the conversation in person, and will opt to reveal their struggle in an email or letter.

Reactions to a trans person's disclosure are as varied as the people doing the reacting. One person might be avidly supportive at first, but experience misgivings later. Another might be averse in the beginning, but gradually come to acceptance. One person might refuse any association with the trans person. Another might become the strongest ally.

Your objective, again, is to listen and learn. Refrain from making judgments and taking sides.

Has this person sought professional help? Attended a trans support group? Gone out in public as the other gender? Already started HRT?

As you demonstrate compassion and a keen desire to learn, hopefully they will feel comfortable telling you every important aspect. Be prepared to hear things you've never heard before, from people who are likely emotionally raw for having suffered in silence, possibly worn out from conversations and confrontations with other important people in their lives, and undoubtedly wary of how you are going to react.

I once had a woman come see me to talk about her marriage. She had seen a Christian counselor. When she described her situation, and what her husband was doing, she told me the counselor looked horrified and declared, "I've never heard such a thing in all my life!" This discouraging response caused her to lose confidence in the person. She went on to describe her situation to me, and yes, it was some shocking stuff. I deliberately kept my reaction neutral, asking questions as appropriate, maintaining tender concern, and trying to ensure the woman felt safe telling her story.

Gender dysphoric persons coming to you will need the same. You can display no shock, no offense. No words of judgment or condemnation can form in your mind so that they might leave your mouth. This is a child of God sitting across from you. Picture the injured lamb which the Lord Jesus is carrying. Be a good shepherd to this wounded sheep.

Unless someone confesses a specific, obvious sin, keep your reaction Gospel-oriented. They need assurance of the Lord's love, that he/she/they is not a freak, or somehow such a sinner that the Lord cannot love he/she/them. Pull out your favorite consolations, the ones that get you through the toughest times, such as the Lord will never leave you nor forsake you (Deuteronomy 31:6, Hebrews 13:5), and His inviting the weary and burdened to Him for rest (Matthew 11:28).

Follow-up sessions

As those who serve in the name of Christ, you provide spiritual care and not talk therapy, unless you are a counselor qualified to provide both. Though the lines become blurred, be keen to remember your vocation. There are many therapists experienced with gender issues. Get to know those in your area. If any gender dysphoric persons have not already sought a therapist, you might be able to assist in locating one. In rural areas, finding a therapist qualified to serve clients with gender identity issues might involve some driving distance or, if feasible, tele-therapy.

There will be a strong likelihood they will need a therapist. If the gender conflict grew serious enough to talk with you, a few conversations—even ongoing spiritual care—will not suffice to ease the angst. Indeed, neither a strong faith nor faithfulness in worship, neither spiritual admonition nor talk therapy, are known to be effective in easing gender dysphoria.

It is important to substantiate the root of the gender conflict. While it is unusual for gender conflict to affect someone who is not transgender, we should never automatically assume the person in front of us actually is transgender. Plus, there might be other concerns—mental or physical—that need to be addressed.

A Christian man reached out to me. He was married to a woman, both in their thirties and members of a non-denominational church. He demonstrated a good knowledge of Scripture and a strong faith in the Lord. He was hurting, thinking that if he didn't transition he was going to burst.

He wanted to live as a woman, but in our communications expressed no internal female sense. After asking many questions, I felt there were some unresolved issues about which he wasn't being forthright. I encouraged him to be honest with his therapist so they could fully and accurately assess his situation.

As you continue to meet with gender dysphoric persons, keep listening, inquiring, and learning.

For those with gender conflict, whether they have recently been gripped by severe dysphoria, or whether they have grappled with it a long time, dozens of factors come into play that affect their ability to cope.

How old are they? Do they live on their own or with family or roommates? Are they in high school or college or employed? Are they married or in a relationship? Do they have children? Do they have support networks? Have the important people in their lives stood by them? Do they have access to therapists? Can they afford therapy? Do they have access to health care? Do they have health insurance and can they afford health care? Do they desire to transition? Have they taken any steps toward transitioning?

Are they suffering suicidal ideation?

Remember the forty-one percent.

Suicide seems the only escape when there are no other exits from suffering. Do an internet search for Leelah Alcorn. Leelah was a teenage trans girl, whose Christian parents' response to her gender plight was to remove her from school, send her to conversion therapy, and limit her access to the outside world. Finding that no one truly heard her, and being forced to live as a boy, when her anguish became too much to bear Leelah stepped in front of a semi-trailer to end her life.

How people treat transgender persons matters. How Christians treat transgender persons matters. Christ is not served when we simply spout Biblical bullet points rather than delve deep to understand the crushing condition that is gender dysphoria and help ease the pain of those suffering it.

Next steps

If their situation has not reached thoughts of suicide, a combination of your spiritual care and a good therapist can relieve some of the immediate stress.

For many with gender dysphoria, the severity of their suffering answers the question whether steps will be taken toward transitioning. It did for me. Everything about transitioning was crazy for who I was in vocation and family and how I lived, but I could no longer abide with the fire in my brain.

Clothes of the identifying gender are the first go-to for many transgender persons, and might be worn for a time in private prior to transitioning publicly. As I mentioned in Chapter Eleven, clothes help ease the distress of incongruity, as they are a highly visible expression that helps align one's external self with the internal sense.

It is a powerful thing, clothing. One feels very differently when dressed in a suit versus sweatpants. Being able to wear clothing typical of the gender with which one identifies is vital to transgender persons. In theory, it seems simple. In practice, it is replete with hindrances.

Trans men (biological females identifying as male), have greater freedom when it comes to dressing in masculine clothes and moving about in the world. We're long accustomed to women wearing short hair styles and male-typical clothing. Stereotypical comments such as "She's quite the tomboy" or "She won't snag a boyfriend looking like that" cut deep and hurt, but there is little danger in a biological female wearing male-typical clothing.

Society is significantly less tolerant of men adopting feminine attire, and those who do so risk being the target of not only humiliating insults, but also physical assault. For this reason, crossdressing in secret has been a necessary solace for many gender dysphoric males.

Clothing, however, has limits in its power to console. For most, it is simply not enough to assuage the dysphoria. Just as talk therapy is not enough. Just as spiritual care is not enough.

The big step

As I experienced my gender dysphoria, I likened it to a slow-growing tumor. It seems an apt comparison, as I've not met anyone for whom their condition stops worsening. The burden of incongruity takes a ruthless path—from incessant aggravation to debilitating affliction.

At some point, the pressure reaches the limits of its confines, and the lid can stay on no more. If you are providing care to a gender dysphoric person, be prepared for the announcement: "I need to transition." How would you react?

What if someone requests to be called by a new name? A new pronoun? Begins dressing and expressing in their identified gender? How would you handle it?

If your default instinct is to lay down the Law, think seventy times seven before you do. If they have reached this point, they have found themselves at the depth of despair, at the end of their rope, and stuck between the rockiest of rocks and the hardest of places. Now, more than ever, the Gospel is what these children of God need as balm for this deep wound of our fallen, fractured nature.

They will need you to remember that this condition is not their choice. They will need you to recognize that no less is at stake than their lives, health, and sanity. They will need you to understand the gravity of their anguish. They will need you to overcome any squeamishness about gender boundaries and grasp their struggle.

A visit from a family member

The same compassion you would have if the trans person were sitting in front of you must be employed when you are meeting with family. They can experience a wide range of emotions when met with the news of a family member's gender identity issue, and throughout the following weeks, months, and years.

Expect to hear a multitude of sentiments:

Confusion. What is gender dysphoria and what does it mean that my child/spouse/parent/sibling has told me they are transgender?

Guilt. Did I do something to cause this? Have I failed as a parent/spouse?

Anxiety. How will this impact us as a family? What does the future hold?

Fear. Will my loved one be safe? Will they be mistreated? What will people think about my family and me?

Frustration. This is all moving so fast, could we just pump the brakes a bit?

Sadness. I feel I'm losing my child/spouse/parent/sibling. How do I cope?

Relief. I knew my loved one was in great pain, now I understand why.

Transgender and the congregation

One of the first questions pastors ask is: if I have a transgender member, how do I introduce this topic to my congregation?

Some congregations have for years been adopting affirming attitudes and are ready for trans members, or already have trans folks in worship. When I was a trans woman, Julie and I were welcomed in a number of congregations as we sought a church home.

But, for a host of churches, transgender persons are seen as sinning. In these congregations, should pastors grasp the reality of gender dysphoria and reckon their transitioning members as Christians in good standing, they will need to be as gentle with their flocks as they have been with the gender dysphoric members.

Whether a church member transitions, or a trans person come into your congregation, controversy might follow. Some will have already made up their minds—"Transitioning is a sin"—and be adamant about the solution—"The transgender person has gotta go." Some will be immensely supportive, no questions asked. In congregations of church bodies that have not been supportive of trans persons, these each tend to be small, albeit highly vocal contingents.

Most will fall in the middle, predominantly unfamiliar with the topic, but aware it is probably a more complex matter than what can be discussed during Sunday morning coffee and donuts. They are wary of confrontation, hoping to avoid the fray, but might genuinely be interested in learning if someone takes the time and initiative to reach them.

I have found more to be empathetic than are willing to be open about it, including pastors. Because this is such a volatile topic, and because the ardent opponents too often resort to hostility and vitriol, those with open minds find they need to keep mum. Many pastors and lay folks surprised me with their support, but who felt they had to do so in private for fear of being excoriated.

In the congregation, start with the basics. Regarding the Christian faith, it cannot be stressed enough that we all are children of Adam, that we all entered the world with Original Sin, that we all live with the many and various—and sometimes extraordinarily unusual—manifestations of our fallen and fractured nature. Then, in equal measure, it must be stressed that Jesus Christ died and lives for all, that every last one of us is saved by grace through faith, not by anything we do. An ongoing proclamation of John 3:16-17 is also encouraged.

Then, educate them with what you learned in this book. Start at the beginning. Cover it all. Give them the foundation needed—the foundation you needed—that they might grasp what gender dysphoria is, that their fellow Christians didn't choose it, and that it is an impossible condition to abide.

Transitioning must be seen as what it is for these hurting Christians—a life-saving avenue for healing. Resolving the dissonance by living in one's identified gender is key to a trans person's survival and sanity. It is the stent to an ailing heart, the splint to a broken bone.

Go slowly. Give them time. Go over the information as many times as needed. Use well the relationship you have built with them. Stress that your care for them is equal to your care for the trans person, and vice versa.

Be prepared for conflict. Strive to maintain calm and compassion among all. Some likely will issue ultimatums—"Either they go or we do"—and even recruit others to join them.

As the body of Christ, we don't work by way of ultimatums. We work by the Golden Rule. We abide in love toward one another.

Your congregation has no doubt already had its share of disagreements and dissension, perhaps about something as minor as carpet color, or something more serious as a budget shortfall. Now, the situation is as critical as it gets; it is the very life and Christian faith of one of their own, a child of God.

In the congregation, the pastor's opinion carries weight. Pastors are in a position to set the proper tone regarding a transgender member. Empathy over judgment. Rationality over antipathy. Wisdom over ignorance. Concern over indifference.

Compassion must govern words and conduct. The Lord Jesus' injured lamb must be tended to; His bruised reed must be nourished.

Caution your congregation to exercise the fruits of the Spirit. Peace. Kindness. Self-control. Encourage them to put forth the best construction. Admonish them not to jump to simplistic conclusions. Reiterate that we all suffer the consequences of Adam's sin and that for many the Fall manifests in difficult physical maladies. Remind them that just because they happened to be born without this affliction doesn't mean they are somehow better or more lovable in the eyes of the Lord.

Emphasize that all—*all*, including the outcasts among us—are saved by grace, freely given through Christ Jesus.

Finally

This matter is not going away. You might not have a transgender member now, but odds are you will in the future. You might not yet have been approached by a family member, neighbor, co-worker, or friend of a transgender person, but odds are you will soon be asked to weigh in.

Despite how confounding and challenging it is to deal with gender dysphoria and transgender, cool heads and compassionate hearts must prevail. The better you prepare your heart and mind to approach this perplexing issue in a Christlike manner, the better you can minister to your sheep—both the wounded and the witnesses.

Gender dysphoric and transgender persons are our brothers and sisters. We're all together in this earthly life. When we are in this as the Church, we are in it together as the body of Christ.

15

Nearly final thoughts

I began this book by telling you how much I value truth and justice, and that I found both lacking in how transgender Christians are treated. In all I have written, I've strived to be true to God's Word and what we presently know about gender dysphoria. For justice, I have appealed to the Gospel of our Lord Jesus Christ.

To help illustrate that many church bodies have a ways to go in their understanding of transgender, I reference two recent writings. Both come from publications of the Lutheran Church—Missouri Synod.

In September 2014, the LCMS's Commission on Theology and Church Relations (CTCR) released *Gender Identity Disorder or Gender Dysphoria in Christian Perspective* (available online). In the document, an excursus on intersex conditions allows for Christians who have ambiguous genitals to make use of hormones and surgery as they strive toward "the greatest possible fullness of service to Christ and others."

This is the easy call. One can view genitals, see what doesn't "match up," and sympathize. As for every other possible reason a person might experience gender conflict—including other less-physically-noticeable intersex conditions—the CTCR finds none of them worthy of being treated medically or socially.

The CTCR opens the section on pastoral care, "A pastoral response to individuals with any form of gender dysphoria requires a clear grounding in a biblically based understanding of natural law and our creation by God as male and female." There it is. Black and white, as if the Fall were able to create intersex conditions of the genitals, but every other experience of gender conflict cannot also be physical in nature.

Ultimately, it seems the CTCR believes "transgender Christian" is an oxymoron. The document states: "If the pastor is caring for a person who is struggling with sexual identity but rejects the Christian church's guidance in this matter, the pastoral task is similar to many other instances of pastoral care in the face of sin and fallenness. Admonition and the call to repentance are needed; some measure of Christian discipline may also become necessary."

Here is how I read that: if Christians transition, they are sinning. If they won't stop, they will be considered unrepentant. That they might recognize the gravity of the matter, they shall be excommunicated from the church.

In the January/April 2015 issue of my seminary's journal, Concordia Theological Quarterly, was an article by my former classmate, Scott Stiegemeyer: *How do you know whether you are a man or a woman?* Of everything I have read from LCMS theologians and pastors, I found Scott to be the most thorough and helpful.

He recognized this: "There is no form of talk therapy or psychotropic medication that can fully assuage the intense dysphoria felt by many transgender patients (page 31)." Where the CTCR would not go so far, he did: "The hypothesis that gender dysphoria is an intersex condition of the mind/brain is consistent with the evidence (page 47)," seeing this as a likely reason psychotherapy and drug therapies don't alleviate gender dysphoria.

With that, where does he land as to transitioning? "Though changing exterior characteristics is easier than changing the brain, this yet does not make the sex-change surgery acceptable. At present, we must conclude that there is simply no medical solution to [gender dysphoria] (page 48)."

How, then, shall a person live with gender dysphoria, at the end of his rope, in agonizing distress, fighting suicidal thoughts?

It is not so simple as "Every gender dysphoric person should transition" just as it is not so simple as "Transitioning is a sin and all transgender people should be excommunicated." As with most deeply complex matters, gray areas fill the bulk of the palette.

In an ideal world, no one would have to transition. Brains and bodies would match. In the event brains and bodies didn't match, there would be no distress over it. In the event there was distress, a quick push of an *easy button* would dissolve it.

But as our ideal world vanished with Adam and Eve chomping a piece of fruit, our fellow Christians suffering from gender dysphoria are faced with figuring out how to survive. For some, this will mean exhausting every possible effort to remain living in their birth sex. Depending upon the person's circumstances and degree of dysphoria, if enough relief can be obtained, this can be a viable option.

It would be my hope that all could achieve such a result, and not have to experience the tumult that transitioning can bring. In reality, though, for many people with gender dysphoria the agony is too great, and taking steps to transition are necessary to ease the anguish.

As with any serious condition, treatment of gender dysphoria should be viewed as a fallen human making use of the Lord's gift of medical science to alleviate the suffering of a fallen body, and not an unrepentant sinner to be banned from Christ's Church.

+ + +

When a person with gender dysphoria has made the decision to transition, remember there is no cookie-cutter approach; each situation and person is unique. There are, however, some important principles and perspectives to keep in mind when a Christian under your care, or a relative of a church member, plans to or has transitioned.

Acknowledging the gravity

Making the decision to transition is not a whimsical notion. While it might seem brash and sudden to an observer, remember that gender dysphoria has been simmering and growing in this person a long time—a lifetime for most.

They are desperately seeking relief.

Recognizing transgender is not a lifestyle

When we lack understanding of something, a quick and flippant way to reflect our disdain is to utter "I don't approve of your lifestyle."

My lifestyle when I was living as a retired transgender woman was exactly the same as my current lifestyle living as a male: rise early, drink a little too much coffee, read the newspapers, write for my blog, spend time with my wife, take care of my grandkids, tend to the lawn and garden, jog five or six miles, cook for my family, try to eat healthy, refrain from harmful activities such as smoking, attend weekly worship, shop for groceries, go out to dinner Saturday evening, be in bed by 10 p.m. This was pretty much my lifestyle prior to being retired, too, except I incorporated those things around the routine of my career.

I know retired folks whose lifestyle is to travel the country in an RV and stay at campgrounds. I know active people whose lifestyle is to be outdoors—hiking, biking, skiing—every chance they get. I know culture lovers whose lifestyle finds them at the opera or symphony on a regular basis. I know sports lovers who religiously buy season tickets and fill their homes with every fan memorabilia they can get their hands on. As a pastor in a small town, I also knew a lot of parishioners whose lifestyle was to go bar-hopping and get drunk several nights a week.

An inherent physiological condition does not a "lifestyle" create. Most transgender people, as with most cisgender people, just want to live normal lives, enjoy God's good earthly gifts, and be good citizens.

Recognizing transgender is not a choice

Being transgender is not a choice, any more than being Italian, or being six-foot-four, or being born with brown hair is a choice. Safely on the outside and comfortably cisgender, some people find it convenient to believe trans people choose their gender identity.

Who chooses intense internal incongruity? Who chooses a condition where discrimination, marginalization, and alienation are the standard result? Who chooses to be the object of scorn and ridicule? Who chooses a situation where you stand a chance of being disowned, evicted, fired, and physically assaulted?

Granted, there will always be the rare bird who insists on being contrary for the sake of being contrary, but such a person uses that tactic as a power play, from a safe position and fully in control. Trans people are in as unsafe and vulnerable a position as there is. By no choice of their own, they find themselves in this spot—a situation with intense internal pressure which, when they seek to release it, creates numerous, equally intense external pressures.

Detransitioning

Most transgender people who have transitioned find their lives improved for having done so. While there are still many obstacles and hurdles along the way, the peace that comes with living in one's identified gender more than compensates for other challenges. A small number of trans people who transitioned as a result of gender dysphoria find they are unable to continue in their identified gender, and they return to living in their birth sex.

The reasons are numerous and varied. A tiny percentage might find they were improperly diagnosed and determined their gender dysphoria was caused by something else. Some might feel their internal sense shift to a different gender identity—perhaps even to a less-defined, neutral feeling of gender. Some might feel compelled—as a result of adverse economic and/or hostile social situations—to live again in their birth sex. Some might have other serious health conditions and they've been unable to find non-discriminatory care as a trans person.

Since transgender found the spotlight in 2015, acceptance of trans persons, though still low, has greatly increased. Transitioning became less stigmatized and more accessible. As with many things, a "jump on the bandwagon" effect might have occurred.

Some persons, especially young adults, have transitioned quickly, endorsed by therapists prone to accelerating a diagnosis of gender dysphoria. The rise in those reporting gender dysphoria, who do not trace it to their childhood, has coined the term *rapid onset gender dysphoria* (ROGD).

Information on ROGD is limited. What professionals are watching is the number of persons returning to living in their birth sex. While the percentage of these detransitioners is small, it is fair to acknowledge, and it demonstrates the importance of leaders in the Church to be informed and educated.

My detransition story is different still, but not unique. Mine was the effect of reversed hormones that altered—with none of my own will or doing—my internal sense of gender. When my hormone levels settled at a level typical of a woman my age, I was left feeling completely male.

I've read blogs of trans persons who medically transitioned and lived for years in their identified gender, yet came to experience themselves as, and resumed living in, their birth sex. Some cannot pinpoint an exact cause for the change in their gender sense.

Ultimately, for the majority who detransition, it is not a "change of mind" about being transgender or a misdiagnosis; rather, it is an internal or external factor that compels the decision.

As with every other hurting Christian facing a difficult life circumstance, trans persons who detransition must be afforded compassion and understanding. "I told you it wouldn't work" doesn't help, always hurts, and never should be heard. It serves nothing and oversimplifies the situation to say "I told you so" or "you're better off now."

Putting statements into context

Refrain from discounting statements and opinions that seem theologically unsound until you've considered the context and motivation. For example, "God made me this way," or "God doesn't make mistakes." For those Christians viewing disorder and brokenness as outside God's perfection and a result of the fall of Adam, statements such as these smack of secularism. Bear in mind that most people aren't making a theological assertion. What they mean and long for others to recognize is "I'm just as valuable a person as the next guy" and "God loves me equally."

Putting motivation into context

Refrain from discounting statements and actions as selfish until you've considered the context and motivation. For example, "I deserve to be happy." While we can all agree that happiness is a worthy goal, we have very different opinions about what methods a person should employ to achieve it. We tend to use the pursuit of happiness clause as justification for self-serving behavior—quitting a job with no backup plan, hitting the bar each night after work instead of going home, buying an impulsive and unbudgeted item, cheating on one's spouse. In cases such as these, if the motivation is giving in to a selfish desire, then "I deserve to be happy" is a pretty flimsy excuse.

When a trans person deciding to transition declares "I deserve to be happy," others affected by the move are quick to portray the decision as selfish. But if we examine the motivation behind the gender dysphoric person's decision to transition, we find the concern is dramatically deeper than simple happiness. For individuals on the brink of despair, they are seeking nothing less than life, sanity, and health. When a gender dysphoric person declares "I deserve to be happy," what they mean is "I don't want to be hurting anymore. I long to be whole."

Respecting names and pronouns

All of the following are commonly spoken to trans persons by their loved ones:

"I named you Samantha and that is what I will always call you."
"If I call you that new name I'm just giving in to your nonsense."
"I'm a creature of habit, I'm used to your old name."
"I keep forgetting to use different pronouns."
"It's too hard for me to make the switch."
"Your voice is low so I naturally want to say he and him."

"I'm too much of a grammar purist to call you they."

Names and pronouns present an exhausting and aggravating battle for trans people. Among all the obstacles to overcome, this is perhaps the most important and personal one for trans people, yet it is so often callously disregarded by the people surrounding them.

Our personal and gender identities permeate our existence—they define the very core of who we are. When you've struggled, long and hard and deep, to stop hiding your inner self and finally live that person outwardly, it is essential that truth, that person, that core being be acknowledged.

Every time an incorrect name or pronoun is uttered, for a trans person it's like being struck by a viper. When we fail to make an effort, when we insist that we know best which names and pronouns to use, when we put our own convenience first, we send this message to trans people: you are not important. You are not valid.

We all want to be treated with dignity and respect. Let us remember how precious the identity of each individual is to our Lord ("See, I have engraved you on the palms of my hands" Isaiah 49:16a, NIV), and grant the same accord to others.

Continuing to learn

Transgender and gender dysphoria are complex issues, and thus require commensurate study. I have read many books on gender dysphoria and living as a transgender person. I believe strongly that every Christian minister, counselor, and church worker should read *Understanding Gender Dysphoria: Navigating Transgender Issues in a Changing Culture* (2015, InterVarsity Press), by Mark Yarhouse PsyD.

Yarhouse explores the topic from a Christian perspective and as a psychologist who has counseled hundreds of transgender persons. His theology fits the profile of my primary audience: those Christians who are prone to getting stuck at "male and female He created them." As Yarhouse quotes transgender Christians, he allows for this to be true: they are transgender and their confession of faith shows they are Christians.

I also commend my memoir to you. I use my story as a framework for the bigger picture of how gender conflict affects transgender persons—from the internal dissonance to the external factors of family, work, church, and society. Where, in this book, I have provided glimpses of myself—such as my church conflict, and the trek with my hormones—in my memoir I provide extensive detail.

Giving the benefit of the doubt to family members

Exercising caution is not necessarily the same as being unsupportive. Transitioning is a big step, and it has consequences—both expected and unintended. While social transitions can be achieved with little physical change, other steps in transitioning, such as hormone therapy and surgeries, can have health risks. It is fair to step back, ask questions, and seek more information.

Sometimes, when family members aren't gung ho in favor of every step being taken as soon as possible, they are branded as dismissive and uncooperative. It is important we discern the difference between caution based on genuine concerns about health and well-being, and opposition born from fear of change and unfamiliarity.

Grief happens

Whereas one relative, friend, or acquaintance might be one-hundred percent on board from day one, another might need more time. Generally, people with gender dysphoria have had a lot more time—even if only internally—to process their situation. The balm to their suffering—transitioning—is obvious to them, and the time frame—immediacy—is a life-saving necessity. As diverse and unique as is each transgender person, the people surrounding them are equally individualized in their personalities, in their reactions, and in how they work through difficult and significant changes.

For transgender people—already battle-worn and emotionally drained—and their allies—eager to help smooth the rough edges for their friend or loved one—it can be hard to abide patiently when others resist giving affirmation.

It is common for people learning about a loved one's gender struggle or intention to transition to experience some or all of the stages of grief. While there is no death involved, one can feel a profound sense of loss by a significant identity of their existence—mom, dad, sister, brother, husband, wife, daughter, son—seemingly disappearing. Also, they might feel apprehensive of an uncertain future. Some, especially parents, might think they are to blame: "What did we do wrong?"

It can take a long time for people to wrap their heads around, and come to terms with, the situation. Recognizing that what others are experiencing is akin to grief can be helpful in trans people and their advocates understanding why their loved ones need time and space.

Mistakes are just that—and we all make them

Just as any number of cisgender people can have bad days, or have difficult personalities, or be rubbed the wrong way, or have life circumstances that lend toward dysfunction, so can trans people.

As cis people can be insensitive, so can trans folks. As cis people are prone to lash out, so are trans folks. Whether cisgender or transgender, people can overreact when another person missteps unintentionally. Too often, though, we are quick to chalk up a trans person's bad behavior as a character flaw, yet treat it as a forgivable mistake in others.

Trans people have tough, emotionally-taxing, adversity-stricken lives, yet they are, at the same time, under the microscope of microscopes. As people who live in a spotlight themselves, and with the expectation of "above reproach" living, pastors and those in the many vocations of Christian service should be able to understand the pressure that goes with this territory. It is unfair to hold trans people to an impossible standard. They are human, and when they make mistakes they should be given the benefit of the doubt just as anyone else.

The Golden Rule is a two-way street

If you are suffering, you want someone to commiserate. If you are sad, you want someone to treat you kindly. If you are ill, you want to be cured. If you slip up, you want to be given a second chance. How quickly this reciprocity flies out the window when we feel we've been wronged or when we disagree with someone. Been on social media much? Attended a heated congregational meeting? Listened to political opposites treat the dinner table as their soapbox?

This is as uphill a battle as there is, instilling an attitude of "do unto others as you would have them do unto you." It is vital that all church leaders, especially pastors, set an example of understanding, civility, and patience, putting the best construction on everything, and encouraging and admonishing the same in others.

Checking in

We know how Christians are. Though they are new creations in Christ and holy in the Father's sight, and are known to do much good a lot of the time, they are still sinners. They will be unfair, hypocritical, and even downright mean. Often, all it takes is for one person to stand out as different—"one of those people"—and that one becomes the Leper of the Month.

Those providing care for trans members will pay attention. In ongoing conversations, they will ask them how it's going with the others in the congregation. Not simply "How are things?" but specifics: "You worked in the kitchen for the spaghetti dinner. Thank you for doing that. How did it go? Were you welcomed? Did you feel you were one of the group?"

Because we Christians are concerned for the whole person, pastors and others in positions of leadership must pay attention to the entire lives of their trans members. Family turmoil can impact a trans person's mental health and ability to function, and even harm their faith in the Lord. Be aware of strained ties, and minister where possible to restore harmony.

Workplace anxieties, economic hardship, and unstable living situations are common problem areas for trans persons. Negativity in the news, such as with bathroom laws and the transgender military service ban, bombard them. Stories of trans people being physically assaulted and killed hit too close to home. Be mindful of the impact adversities have on a trans person.

And then checking in some more

I can imagine some folks mumbling that trans Christians need a lot of care.

Yes, they do.

Trans persons need a lot of care, just as does the family whose loved one died tragically. Just as does the one going through months or years fighting a disease. Just as does the one who continues to mourn a divorce. Just as do the parents of a special-needs child.

The day after I told one of my daughters about my gender dysphoria, she commented, "It's hard being a person."

Yes, it is.

You, the persons in position of caring for your fellow Christians, are needed by them to be the challenging-to-translate German word that Lutherans love for pastors: *seelsorger.* My preferred definition is *curer of souls.* When you have this attitude, that your work in the stead of the Good Shepherd is curer of souls, you will always bear in mind it is hard being a person, and you will find it your privilege to come alongside your struggling people, for their temporal and eternal good.

+ + +

Justin (the young man from Chapter Ten) called one evening in July 2019. We had not spoken for a couple of months. He had taken the plunge and begun HRT. He was now more than two months into it, so I expected him to be feeling the physical effects.

Would he be experiencing the calm that often comes by this point? I was so hoping he was feeling a bit better.

Nope.

He'd not contacted me because work and family had him busy. Despite plenty to keep him distracted from his gender conflict, it was as bad as ever. Finally, more than half a year into knowing Justin, and in almost every conversation asking him if he ever wished he were dead, he had now reached that point.

"Do you have a plan?" I asked. "No," he began. "But there are times when I simply wish I were not alive. That it would be better to be dead."

He continued, "When Jenny married me, she had expectations." He paused. He'd come to tears and couldn't talk, so I filled in the rest: "She had married a guy, and she expected always to be married to a guy." "Yeah," came his softly spoken reply.

Justin sees three paths. Two are realistic. Only one looks good. The first realistic one is he keeps on as he has for his entire life. Never comfortable with himself. Growing worse.

The second realistic path is he will transition. When he contemplates that path, a dozen other paths open up. All of them appear replete with trouble.

The third path is taking his life. He doesn't see himself taking that route … but who knows what a person might do should push come to shove?

Our conversation grew long. I never let our discussions end without encouraging him with the Gospel, so I spoke of the Lord Jesus' love for him.

Less than a week later, Justin's name again popped up on my ringing phone. He was crying. He was hurting worse than the previous conversation. Soon, we were crying together, my feeling his pain through the remembrance of my own, neither of us with any answer to this imprisoning, bedeviling gender conflict.

"I don't want to transition," his voice shaking with emotion. "I don't want to be transgender."

I had been encouraging him to call his pastor. He was hesitant. He didn't know whether his pastor had any knowledge of gender issues, nor his attitude about them. I had previously offered to call the man on his behalf, to break the ice, keeping Justin anonymous. I repeated my offer. Justin now took me up on it, so the next day I gave the pastor a call.

The pastor demonstrated keen understanding. He spoke with compassion about a trans teen in his congregation. Soon, Justin called the pastor to set up a visit. Thankfully, he now has in-person spiritual care.

Back to the phone call with Justin, finally, there was silence. I searched my mind for a Gospel passage. Without thinking, I began reciting, "The Lord is my shepherd, I shall not want ..." Finishing the psalm, I said, "You, Justin, will dwell in the house of the Lord, forever. Your Jesus walks with you through this valley of the shadow of death. He is faithful. He will always be with you, and you will always be with Him."

16

The properly-purpose-driven pastor

Pastors, you lead the congregation. While all readers of this book can be encouraged in this chapter, I write this directly to you pastors.

I once began a sermon, "Christianity is a religion of doing things. You know, we are to be doing the commandments, and treating others the way we want them to treat us." I went on, building my case.

I noticed a woman near the back of the church. She stood out because she was shaking her head. Slowly. Frowning. Sending me the message: "No, pastor. This doesn't sound right."

She was on to me. I was setting up the congregation.

What I was saying sounded right—of course, we are to obey the commandments, do good works, mind our mouths—but my focus was wrong. I was talking about the by-products of being Christians, erroneously making them paramount.

I've heard a lot of sermons, from a lot of pastors. Far too many sermons contain little or no proclamation of the Gospel. Some preachers never even mention the name of Jesus, while others talk about Him only because He is the leading man of the text. The worst sermons only reference "God"—the generic equivalent of my referring to my wife Julie as "person"—and then only for the purpose of some moralism or lesson in holy living.

Is the focus of living as a Christian to be a constant striving toward righteous behavior? Or is our focus to be the righteousness of the Lord Jesus by which we live in God's love toward Him and our neighbor?

The work of pastors is not to make good little boys and girls of the members of their churches. While pastors will guide their flocks in living righteously so as to glorify God—as the Lord Jesus says, that others might see our good deeds and give glory to God the Father (Matthew 5:16)—pastors' ultimate work is to proclaim Jesus Christ and Him crucified, to so preach and teach the Good News of the Lord Jesus' work that the people live in Christ, that they put their hope fully and only in Christ, that they have the sure and certain hope they belong to Him, now and forever.

+ + +

Before I went to seminary, I was in sales. We were a small company; I received little training aside from learning the basics of our product.

Early on in the job, I encountered a customer who taught me a lesson that made me a true salesman. It was simple: tell me about your product, but also tell me what it does for me. Sell the steak *and* the sizzle—that is, prove to me why I want this particular steak.

Pastors are good at proclaiming the steak of the Gospel—that Jesus died for our sins—but are often lacking in declaring the sizzle—that Jesus has reconciled us to God the Father, that we are children of God and coheirs with Christ, that our faith in Christ is a sure and certain hope of being resurrected from the dead to a life in which there will be no more death, or mourning, or crying, or pain, that though we keep on sinning God the Father delights in us His precious children.

When I became a Lutheran and comprehended not just the substantive steak, but also the sweet sizzle of the Gospel, it propelled me into the ministry. I could not not be proclaiming the Gospel.

In seminary, a classmate warned that we not shorthand the Gospel. To shorthand the Gospel is to say things such as "You were saved at Calvary," or "Take your sins to the cross," and believe you've sufficiently proclaimed the Gospel. To shorthand the Gospel is to assume your hearers know what those statements mean. To shorthand the Gospel requires your hearers to fill in the blanks.

How many people have argued, "My family doesn't need me to tell them I love them. They know." Ah, but how sweet is it to hear "I love you"? How wonderfully filled are our hearts when a loved one further tells us what it is they love about us?

We know who loves us, and we know the Gospel. But we need to hear both—fully and generously. We need the sizzle!

Here are a few of the Scriptures that filled my heart and sizzled for me, beginning with Colossians chapter one. The Spirit had Paul inform us as John had done to begin his Gospel, that everything was created by the Word, the Son of God. But the Spirit had more to reveal, and Paul now wrote it: not only was everything created *through* the Son, but everything was created *for* the Son (Colossians 1:16).

As much as learning the Gospel changed me, this was especially profound for me. I was made for the Son of God, just as everything was made for Him. The reason it was the Son who became man to pay for our sins is because we are God the Father's gift to His Son, and since the Son's love for His Father is perfect He could do nothing else than to save this creation.

To save me.

I'm that important to Him.

And I am that important to Him no matter what transpires in my life. And while I always preface the next thought with, "This doesn't mean I can do whatever I please," I always come back to, "His love for me remains perfect"—even when a struggle that defies the imagination of most people, such as one's dealing with gender dysphoria by transitioning, disrupts our lives.

When I was living as a trans woman, the same seminary classmate who warned that we not shorthand the Gospel said to Julie and me, "Whether you take the route to the left, or take the one to the right, you belong to the Lord."

While we were still sinners, Christ died for us (Romans 5:8). While we were fallen and broken, dead in our transgressions (Ephesians 2:5)—indeed, enemies of God (Colossians 1:21)—Christ died for us.

The Lord Jesus didn't direct us to get our act together before He would act.

He doesn't even demand that we get our act together after we are enlightened with His gifts and trust Him as our Lord. He calls us to love—both Him and our neighbor—yet when we fail to love He doesn't remove His love from us. When we are unfaithful, He remains faithful.

When I transitioned and lived as a transgender person, this truth sustained me, that I belong to Christ and He remains faithful to me in His love. When Julie and I were rejected by the church body we love, this truth sustained us.

There were times I was on the verge of hating Jesus. I screamed prayers of despair, of pleading, *"Please, stop all of this! I hate being this way! What are you doing to me? What are you thinking? This is all so crazy! I am an offense to many! They call me a freak and mentally unstable and giving in to temptation! People tell me I'm going to hell! Get me out of this mess!"*

I bawled and thrashed and wailed. Until I wore myself out.

It happened every few weeks.

For five years.

Every time, either later that day or by the next day, the Lord refreshed me. He strengthened my spirit. He gave me the ability to see Him, to trust Him, to remember and know that I belong to Him, that He will not fail me.

That He would get me through this, until He gets me to heaven.

Another truth affects me as deeply as knowing I was made for my Lord Jesus. Opening the epistle to the Ephesians, the Spirit revealed that we who are holy and blameless in God's sight were chosen before anything was created, indeed that the Lord predestined us to be adopted children through Jesus Christ (Ephesians 1:4-5).

Wow! Not only was I made for the Son, I was chosen to have faith in the Son before anything was created. This passage informs me: I am so important to the Lord that before He did anything else He chose me to be His own.

It's no accident I am a Christian: *one who belongs to Christ.* This was the Lord's purpose, from the beginning of the beginning.

When Ephesians chapter one was the Sunday epistle lesson—often, the first Sunday of the new year—I always preached on it. I used it to reinforce this truth in the people commended to my care, that they might take into the new year the sure and certain knowledge of who they are.

There's more. In John ten and Romans eight we are strengthened in the blessed truth that no one can snatch us out of the Lord Jesus' hand (John 10:28), that nothing in all of creation can separate us from God's love for us in Christ (Romans 8:38-39).

It should be no surprise the Lord Jesus won't let anything or anyone else have me. I was made for Him. Before the creation of the world I was chosen to belong to Him. He gave His life for me, for pity's sake—He's going to let some earthly trouble or sin or illness or turmoil win a victory over Him?

All of this is the sizzle which emanates from the steak which is Christ's crucifixion and resurrection. And though we Christians keep on sinning, and though we keep finding ourselves in sticky situations, and though we continue to think selfish things, and speak hurting words, and venture down wrong paths, we still belong to Jesus.

Whether it is a gender dysphoric or transgender person, or anyone whose situation might tempt him to accept worldly thinking over God's Word, pastors' work is to teach the faith so their members bear their problems in a God-fearing, Christ-glorifying manner; so they rely solely on the finished work of Jesus Christ and not on a Christian's attaining a certain level of sanctification.

It's hard being a Christian. We live in a world where secular humanism is king, where earthly ideas hold sway over God's Word, where "eat, drink, and be merry" is the all-too-common motto for life.

The competition for the Christian's mind is fierce. While no pastors want to concede anything, they know their people often hold ideas and philosophies that are in direct opposition to church doctrine.

The goal of pastors is not to use God's Word to create perfect Christians, whose every thought, word, and deed are as Adam's when the Lord created him. If this is the goal, every pastor will fail one-hundred percent of the time.

The goal of pastors is to proclaim the Word of God so their members hold onto dear Jesus. So when each one dies and they officiate their funerals, they can have confidence commending their remains to the Lord "in the sure and certain hope of the resurrection to eternal life."

As a pastor, I officiated 150 funerals. At every one I read Job 19. "I know that my Redeemer lives." "In the end He will stand upon the earth." "After my flesh has been destroyed I will see Him with my own eyes."

I came to say that if you can find anyone else who has beaten death through resurrection, never again to be prone to death, go ahead and put your faith in that person. You won't find him or her. No one else has done it, except for Jesus Christ. And, because Jesus has defeated the one enemy common to all people, when He says He will defeat that enemy for you and me, too, we are wise to listen to Him.

Just as Jesus' death would have been for nothing without His resurrection, so our deaths are nothing without our own resurrection. And it will not be until we are resurrected that we finally will have every trouble resolved.

The blind will have their sight restored. The lame will run freely. The infirm will be filled with perfect health. And transgender persons will be whole in the sex which the Lord intended for them.

Pastors, it's your privilege to console those whose gender struggles have them nearly tearing their flesh off themselves, and to encourage in Christ those who have transitioned who face continual conflict with family and church and workplace and society.

It's your privilege to speak every last wonderful bit of Jesus to them. That these hurting ones belong to Jesus. That the Lord chose them before the creation of the world to be holy in His sight. That they were made for Jesus. That Jesus died for them. That Jesus lives for them.

That Jesus won't let anything come between them and Him. Not now. Not ever.

+ + +

Dear brothers and sisters in Christ, in whatever capacity you work in service to the Lord Jesus, you do the most important work on earth.

It's your privilege to proclaim the One who is the Creator and Savior, the One for whom *you* were created, the One in whom *you* were chosen, the One with whom *you* will live forever in the paradise of the new creation.

The Lord be with you, now and forever. Amen.

17

Epilogue

It was mid February. Justin and I hadn't talked since the arrival of 2020. He texted, eager to talk and share.

He'd made an appointment with an endocrinologist to restart HRT, which he had stopped last summer. Justin now was prepared to transition.

He finally had enough of the suffering. Striving to be male wasn't helping. Striving to appreciate the role of husband and father had no effect. Pastoral care, talk therapy, placing himself in the hands of the Lord—nothing eased the gender conflict. It only grew worse.

Jenny wasn't surprised at the news. She realized it was coming, witnessing Justin's ups and downs, and impossible-to-conceal pain. Justin said she took it well, that she is on board.

He also told his pastor—the minister with whom I had spoken.

It was difficult for Justin to break this news to his pastor. Remember, both Justin's father and father-in-law are pastors. There is nothing in Justin's life or upbringing that would have a place for the news he was about to reveal.

He said the words, "I need to transition. I need to see if it will help me," and broke down. As a true *seelsorger*, a curer of souls, the pastor uplifted Justin with words of assurance. Of the Gospel. Of the Lord Jesus' love for him.

As he spoke, again and again Justin broke down. Every time, the pastor responded with words of mercy and grace.

"When I couldn't speak, he always had the right response. He encouraged me. He spoke of God's love for me. Everything he said was helpful and kind."

For Justin, many hurdles dot the road ahead—telling parents, family, and friends; deciding when to adopt a new name and pronouns; approaching management and colleagues at work.

The entirety of it is daunting times intimidating. Yet, for the first time in the year we've known each other, Justin sounded hopeful. And, despite the trials, Justin will at least have a pastor who will uplift and sustain with the love of Christ Jesus.

Throughout our chat, one Bible verse stayed in my mind. It's a promise from the Lord that sustained me through my years of trial.

"Justin, in Romans 8:28, the Lord promises to work all things for the good of those who love Him. How many things does He promise to work for our good?"

"Everything," replied Justin. "Every. Single. Thing."

"That's right. Not just a lot of things. Not many things. All things. He is faithful to those who love Him, whom He has called according to His purpose.

"His purpose is to give us eternal life, through our Lord Jesus. His purpose is for us to show the world we belong to Him by how we live our lives. When I transitioned, that was my determination, to show I was the same child of God I had always been.

"And that is what you will do, Justin. And many will benefit by how you live as a Christian."

"Yeah," said Justin. "Amen."

Printed in Great Britain
by Amazon